**HEALTH** REPORTS:
DISEASES AND DISORDERS

# ANXIETY DISORDERS

BRUCE M. HYMAN, Ph.D.,
& CHERRY PEDRICK, R.N.

TWENTY-FIRST CENTURY BOOKS
MINNEAPOLIS

Note: Some of the material in Chapter Two appeared in a different form in
*Obsessive-Compulsive Disorder*, by Bruce M. Hyman and Cherry Pedrick, © 2011
by Bruce M. Hyman and Cherry Pedrick.

Twenty-First Century Books
A division of Lerner Publishing Group, Inc.
241 First Avenue North
Minneapolis, MN 55401 U.S.A.

Website address: www.lernerbooks.com


Library of Congress Cataloging-in-Publication Data

Hyman, Bruce M.
        Anxiety disorders / by Bruce M. Hyman and Cherry Pedrick.
            p.   cm. — (USA Today health reports: Diseases and disorders)
        Includes bibliographical references and index.
        ISBN 978-0-7613-6084-1 (lib. bdg. : alk. paper)
        1. Anxiety disorders—Juvenile literature. 2. Neuroses—Juvenile literature.
    I. Pedrick, Cherry. II. Title.
    RC531.H982 2012
    616.85'22—dc23                                               2011021426

Manufactured in the United States of America
1 – DP – 12/31/11

# CONTENTS

**USA TODAY**
**HEALTH** REPORTS:
DISEASES AND DISORDERS

# LIVING WITH ANXIETY

Fear is a normal, healthy part of the human experience. It is an appropriate response to threats, challenges, and potential loss. Every day, fear encourages you to study harder for tests, reminds you to get college applications in on time, and makes you take reasonable safety precautions. When fear is excessive, out of proportion to the threats, and causes excessive worry about future events that are not likely to happen, the result is anxiety. When anxiety persists and interferes with daily life, an anxiety disorder may be diagnosed. The young people you'll meet in this book have struggled with anxiety. You may feel that you know one or more of them, but they are actually representative of many teens who live with anxiety disorders. The teens discussed below display only a small sampling of the features of that disorder. Your anxiety disorder may not appear similar to any of these, and that's OK.

## CAROL: PANIC DISORDER WITH AGORAPHOBIA

*College was absolutely out of the question. Carol felt that it was all she could do just to leave the house with her best friend or her parents. She'd had a horrible episode of panic at the mall several months ago. Out of nowhere, she suddenly felt her heart racing, extreme tightness in her chest, and shortness of breath. Dizzy and trembling, she stumbled to a bench to catch her breath, convinced she was having a heart attack. After several minutes, she finally calmed down and called her parents from her cell phone. Carol was afraid to drive, so her parents came to the mall to get her. Her mother took care of Carol, while her father drove Carol's car back home. Graduation from high school can be an exciting but nerve-racking time, and Carol had been busy preparing for it. Carol's panic episode was probably just nerves, her mother suggested.*

The following week, Carol had another episode of panic while working in the yard, and her parents took her to the doctor. The doctor ran tests, all of which turned out negative. Because there was nothing wrong with Carol's physical health, the doctor concluded that these episodes were panic attacks. Carol never knew when she would have one, and there seemed to be no warning or reason for them. Determined to avoid these very frightening feelings and sensations, she began to stay home as much as possible. She went out only with someone she could depend on to get help for her if she should have a panic attack.

A doctor can help assess whether symptoms associated with a panic attack are those of an anxiety disorder or of another condition.

## MAGGIE: SOCIAL PHOBIA

For Maggie, home had always represented safety and security, perhaps much more so than for most people. She remembered the extreme fear she felt as a little girl when her mother left her with a babysitter or at preschool. She felt abandoned and lost. Most children cried for a few minutes and then became interested in a favorite toy or found a friend to play with. Maggie would cry until it seemed there were no tears left to cry and then sleep for a few minutes and play quietly by herself. Throughout her school years, she made two close friends. But she had been too shy to join clubs or get involved in sports.

Maggie's shyness as a child and fear of being away from her parents limited her ability to feel comfortable in social situations with other children. As an awkward teen, she was filled with fear of what others might think of her. Just the thought of being called on in class made her nervous and kept her awake at night. Conversations with boys made her so nervous that her palms got sweaty and her mouth became so dry she could hardly talk. She always felt certain that she'd make a fool of herself.

## JOSÉ: SOCIAL PHOBIA

José was known around school as one of the smartest students. He excelled in history, English, and science. As a star on the debate team, he had won statewide awards for his speaking and debating skills. At an all-state debate championship, he spoke about the role of affirmative action in college admissions. During his argument, he suddenly found himself staring at the audience. To José, it seemed as if thousands of expectant faces were staring at him, waiting for him to say something. He opened his mouth, but nothing came out.

Feeling dizzy, he grasped the lectern and closed his eyes. José opened his eyes and looked down at his notes and then out at the audience. It wasn't thousands of people, only thirty students and teachers in the audience. He began to present his arguments again. But he blanked out after a few sentences, stuttered, and apologized. The people in the room seemed to be stunned in silence. He felt a rush of fear and embarrassment. He wanted to run from the room.

Over the coming weeks and months, José's fear of debating and of any type of public speaking grew. While previously self-assured and talkative in class, he became timid and fearful of opening his mouth. He was afraid that he'd forget something important or stutter. Before debates, he felt dizzy and sweaty, his heart racing in anticipation. His mouth would become dry, and he'd feel so nauseated he could hardly eat for days before a debate.

## HOLLY: SPECIFIC PHOBIA

Holly had once read in a nature book that bee stings could be poisonous to some people. One year while camping, Holly was walking along a trail when she heard buzzing around her head. She looked quickly from side to side but didn't see anything. Then she felt something on her forehead. Without thinking, she slapped her head with her hand, smashing a bee as it stung her. Reeling from the pain of the sting, she recalled in a flash what she had once read about bee stings and became overwhelmed with panic. The sting resulted in some pain and swelling in her face, but after a trip to the doctor and taking some medication, Holly was okay.

The story of Holly's bee sting was often told in the family, and everyone laughed. They also laughed about how she frantically waved her arms around when any type of flying insect came anywhere near her. Holly stayed away from places where bees might exist. She never walked in the woods or forests near her home, worked in the garden, went camping or fishing, or even visited the local zoo for fear of being near the insect exhibit.

## JAKE: OBSESSIVE-COMPULSIVE DISORDER

What if he didn't wash his hands well enough or often enough? How often and how much was enough? Jake no longer knew. He washed his hands at least one hundred times a day. He took forty-five-minute

Obsessive-compulsive disorder is an anxiety disorder characterized by repeating certain behaviors such as washing hands.

showers three times a day. Jake washed his hands at the mere thought that there was even the remotest possibility he'd touched an object with germs or a surface with a toxic chemical coating it. The thought of it just terrified him. Jake had obsessive-compulsive disorder. Washing his hands for the normal twenty seconds was enough at first. But after a while, it just didn't relieve his anxiety and distress. He would wash each finger separately, often counting to his favorite number—9— before moving on to the next digit. It had to be done perfectly. Often the moment he finished drying his hands, he'd feel a rush of fear and uncertainty that the job was not done just right, and he'd need to wash again. The bad thoughts would return over and over, with each repetitive hand wash leaving his hands looking raw and chapped.

## PAUL: POST-TRAUMATIC STRESS DISORDER

Paul's life was forever changed when a fire destroyed his family home and took the life of one of his sisters. He spent a month in the hospital recovering from his burns. His father and two brothers were also hospitalized with injuries. Everyone said that if it hadn't been for Paul, they might not have made it out alive. He was the first one to smell the smoke and awaken everyone. He got his brothers out of the house and was on his way back to get his sister when the smoke and flames stopped him, and he passed out. He couldn't remember much of that night during his waking hours, but he'd wake up screaming with nightmares. This was embarrassing to him, and he often felt weak and foolish. Paul had trouble sleeping at night and began to avoid going to bed, afraid of the dreams.

Before the fire, Paul was active in school activities. Afterward, he began to withdraw and stayed home most of the time. His parents tried to get him to talk about the fire, but he'd get upset when it was mentioned. Paul's symptoms continued for several months.

## ROSA: ACUTE STRESS DISORDER

As Rosa was walking from her car to the entrance of the library one evening, she was attacked from behind. She barely saw the man's face as he snatched her purse and ran. Rosa was stunned for a few seconds and then screamed. Soon people from the library ran to her aid. They called the police, and Rosa gave them a statement. Her parents and little brother arrived. They took her to urgent care. There, doctors confirmed that one of Rosa's fingers had been broken from the force of the mugger yanking Rosa's purse out of her hand. Otherwise, Rosa was physically uninjured.

At the police station the next day, Rosa looked through folders of mug shots but couldn't identify her attacker. It was dark when the man mugged her, and he had been wearing a hooded sweatshirt. At first, Rosa didn't seem too bothered by the incident. She wasn't hurt much, and she had only a few dollars in her purse. Her parents were supportive. They reminded her that while things such as money can be replaced, she couldn't be.

When things settled down, Rosa began to think about the mugging. The memories would flood back without warning. She remembered her intense fear. Could something even worse happen? She began to startle easily and had difficulty concentrating on her homework. Most of all, Rosa couldn't get the look on her little brother's face that night out of her mind. When her family took her to urgent care, he'd looked so scared. What if she'd been hurt badly? What if the man had pulled a gun or a knife? She could have been killed. What would that have done to her little brother? And wasn't the attack due to her own carelessness? She could have gone to the library with a friend. She could have gone earlier, during the day. She should have worn a shoulder bag instead of carrying a purse in her hand. To make things worse, she realized she could have been mugged no matter what precautions she'd taken.

Rosa withdrew from her activities for a week after the incident, preferring to stay home. The world just seemed too dangerous. Her parents encouraged her to go out with her friends. Her brother told her how proud he was of his brave big sister. She could see that the experience wasn't leaving a scar on him. He even seemed more confident, and they seemed to have a stronger relationship. Gradually, Rosa resumed her normal activities. She took a few extra precautions when she went out, but the fearfulness she felt at first went away after a couple of weeks.

## ELIZABETH: GENERAL ANXIETY DISORDER

"Don't worry!" Elizabeth was tired of hearing this. Everyone was always telling her to stop worrying and with good reason—she was always worrying. About everything! She spent hours thinking about *all the things that could go wrong. Some of the disasters she imagined were very real and possible, just not very likely. For example, her parents could get divorced, she could fail all of her classes, or someone in her family could get sick or injured. Elizabeth's other worries weren't really about disasters: something could go wrong at a party, she could fail a test, or someone's feelings could get hurt.*

*Elizabeth felt constantly tense and often had difficulty sleeping. She saw the doctor about stomachaches and headaches. The doctor told her she had migraines, but she worried that something even more serious was wrong with her. She could not get the thought of having a brain tumor out of her mind.*

## FEAR VS. ANXIETY

Fear is a response to a well-defined danger, a specific object or situation. Think of it as your brain's natural alarm reaction to a true threat or danger. The level of fear one experiences is in proportion to the actual threat. Common fears include fear of illness, job loss, physical harm, poverty, and death. Anxiety, as opposed to fear, is an excessive, out-of-proportion response to a vague, ill-defined, future-oriented danger. You may not even be able to describe the actual threat.

Anxiety affects people on three levels. *Physically*, you can have many symptoms, including rapid heart rate, stomach discomfort (butterflies), trembling, nausea, muscle tightness, sweating, and shortness of breath. *Mentally*, you might have uneasiness, worry, intrusive thoughts, confusion, poor concentration, and a sense of helplessness. *Behaviorally*, you may avoid particular objects, places, or situations. As in obsessive-compulsive disorder, you may perform unnecessary rituals. As you'll see, recovery often involves treatment of the physical, mental, and behavioral aspects of the symptoms.

May 8, 2007

From the Pages of USA TODAY

# Brooding weighs on mind and body

Mulling over the past, stewing about problems, dissecting every little remark your boss makes, worrying about the future. These mental habits take a toll on the body, according to cutting-edge research on the biology of brooding.

Humans are the only species prone to "overthinking" that solves nothing, says Julian Thayer, a psychologist at Ohio State University. New studies suggest that those who ruminate a lot may have higher blood pressure and heart rates, less effective immune systems, surges of stress hormones that strain the heart, more depression and perhaps even shorter life spans.

Everyone experiences stress, but chronic brooders prolong and amplify their stress, says psychologist Nicholas Christenfeld of the University of California-San Diego.

He gives adults stressful or frustrating tasks in his studies, then checks what happens to the bodies of those who either ruminate a lot afterward or don't. The original stress causes heart rate and blood pressure to rise, but people who don't fret afterward come down to their original, healthier levels much more quickly than those who keep stewing, Christenfeld says.

Vigorous exercise and even listening to soothing classical music also speed physical recovery, so distraction may prevent harmful effects in the short term, he says.

Still, those who often react to stress by brooding have less of a blood pressure drop overnight than people who usually let go of things, shows a new study by psychologist Brenda Key of the University of Calgary [in Canada]. Smaller-than-normal dips in blood pressure at night have been linked to a higher risk of dying from strokes and heart attacks, she adds.

Other research finds that dwelling on an unpleasant experience increases the release of chemicals that can weaken the immune system over time; this may hamper someone's ability to fight illness, Christenfeld says. Increases in the stress hormone cortisol after rumination also can hinder the immune system and contribute to cardiovascular disease, he says.

There's no proof that chronic overthinkers die sooner because of it, Christenfeld says. But one new study suggests that may be the case, at least for men. The study began with more than 1,600 men ages 40 to 90. At the start, they were given personality tests. They were tracked for 17 years to see how a trait called neuroticism affected survival.

Those who score high in the neurotic trait are "worrywarts" who cope poorly with stress and tend to be highly anxious or depressed, says study leader Daniel Mroczek of Purdue University [in Indiana]. "They don't let things roll off their backs."

Among men who were high in this trait at the start and became even more so over time, half had died 17 years after the study started. Among those who were high in neuroticism at the start but didn't increase, and the less neurotic, 75% to 85% were still alive. The good news: "People can change," Mroczek says. "If you learn to worry or fret less, you may add time to your life." But the findings apply only to men, he emphasizes.

Women are more likely than men to overthink, says psychologist Susan Nolen-Hoeksema of Yale University [in Connecticut], who has studied rumination for years. Women brood about things that make them sad or anxious; men are more likely to stew about anger, she says.

And you don't have to be an adult to suffer bad health effects. In her latest, four-year study of adolescent girls, she found that girls prone to ruminating were more likely than the others to develop eating disorders, alcohol problems and depression. Future chronic ruminators often were anxious little kids, Nolen-Hoeksema says.

The science of how overthinking affects bodies is still young, says William Gerin of Columbia College of Physicians and Surgeons. "But so far we've learned that if you catch yourself ruminating a lot, it's probably contributing to unhappiness and physical health problems as well.

"It's not the stress that kills us, it's how we respond to it."

### How to quit your worrying

Many people overthink because they're trying to solve problems or get over life traumas, says Stephen Lepore, a public-health researcher at Temple University [in Pennsylvania].

But other methods are more effective. Writing one's deepest feelings about stressful experiences can improve health "and take the sting out. It acts like a buffer."

People who worry too much also can try these methods recommended by Yale University psychologist Susan Nolen-Hoeksema:

- Seek out new friends who prefer to help solve problems rather than indulge in mutual hand-wringing.
- Meditate or pray regularly.
- Schedule limited "overthink" sessions; don't do it any other time.
- Work on forgiveness and lowering unrealistically high expectations.

*—Marilyn Elias*

Why do we become anxious? It starts with the brain/body's natural fear response to perceived threats. Our senses of sight, hearing, touch, taste, and smell pick up signs of danger in our environment. The brain evaluates the information and begins a process that prepares the body for fight or flight. It's the same process that prepared our ancestors to run from an attacking grizzly bear or to stay and fight the bear to the end. The threats and dangers of our modern society, while not the same as attacking grizzly bears, involve threats to our self-worth, our self-esteem, our sense of personal security, our health, and the safety of ourselves and those we love. While this is a far cry from attacking grizzly bears, our brain doesn't know the difference.

Certain areas of the brain analyze incoming information and control emotions. When a threat is perceived, an activating chemical called adrenaline is released throughout the body. Adrenaline causes the heart to race, blood pressure to rise, and breathing to quicken. When this response helps you flee a burning building, perform at your best, study extra hard for a test, or prepare thoroughly for a race, the response is healthy and protective. A healthy fear response furthers your survival and helps you do your best. Gone too far, however, fear becomes unhealthy and has the opposite effect on performance.

It's useful to think of anxiety as the brain's healthy fear response gone haywire. Anxiety is what occurs when the brain's fight-or-flight mechanism becomes mistakenly associated in our minds with objects, places, people, situations, or ideas that we don't normally think of as very threatening. For example, if you were swimming in the ocean and saw a black fin rise out of the water a few feet from you, and the lifeguard hollered, "Shark in the water!" your heart would start racing. You would gasp for air and start rapidly thrashing your arms to get as far away from the shark as quickly as possible. Imagine having that same heart-pumping, "Got to get away right now!" reaction not only in the presence of a real shark but at a movie about sharks, looking at a picture of sharks, seeing any fish that resembles a shark, or just being within a few feet of the ocean.

Reactions like these are what behavioral scientists sometimes refer to as the brain's "false alarms." Despite that no true shark threat is present, the brain's fight-or-flight reaction is triggered anyway, causing great distress and avoidance. These false alarms become learned and ingrained by the repeated association of the fearful situation (bees, zoos, heights, door locks, blood, etc.) with the brain's fight-or-flight response. They are the basis of all anxiety disorders.

## WHAT CAUSES ANXIETY DISORDERS?

More than 16 percent of the U.S. teen and adult population, or 20 to 23 million Americans, have some type of anxiety disorder. Science is providing more and more solid clues in the search for greater understanding of the causes of anxiety disorders. Our best knowledge to date points to the idea that anxiety disorders are caused by a multitude of factors—biological, genetic, psychological, and environmental.

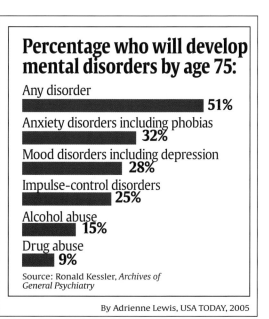

**Percentage who will develop mental disorders by age 75:**

Any disorder
**51%**

Anxiety disorders including phobias
**32%**

Mood disorders including depression
**28%**

Impulse-control disorders
**25%**

Alcohol abuse
**15%**

Drug abuse
**9%**

Source: Ronald Kessler, *Archives of General Psychiatry*

By Adrienne Lewis, USA TODAY, 2005

Each factor contributes in varying degrees to a person's unique vulnerability to developing an anxiety disorder.

It appears that some people genetically inherit from their parents extra-sensitive fight-or-flight warning systems. They seem to be born alert, nervous, or worried. Their bodies over-respond to harmless stimuli as if they were true dangers. Studies of the genetics of identical twins have demonstrated how anxiety disorders tend to run in families. Identical twins have exactly the same genetic make-up. Several studies have shown that when an identical twin has an anxiety disorder, the other twin is more likely to have an anxiety disorder. This is less likely with fraternal (nonidentical) twins. So it appears that our genetic makeup plays a role in the development of an anxiety disorder.

Other factors enter the picture soon after we're born. After all, if it were all up to our genes, identical twins would have a 100 percent chance of having the same anxiety disorders. Since that isn't the case, we know that other factors are very much involved. Our environment, upbringing, and stress can combine to make it more or less likely that we'll develop a specific anxiety disorder.

Besides genetics, certain medical conditions can cause symptoms of anxiety and panic. These include some heart diseases, mitral valve prolapse, emphysema, inner-ear disturbance, menstrual and menopausal conditions, food additive allergies, hypoglycemia, hyperthyroidism, and deficiencies of calcium or magnesium. Treating these conditions often eases the anxiety. Withdrawal from alcohol or drugs can also cause anxiety and panic. A person can have anxiety as a reaction to cocaine, amphetamines, and other stimulants such as caffeine or ephedra.

Some people can find evidence of anxiety disorders within many branches of their family tree. Others can point to traumas or severe childhood neglect or abuse in the development of their anxiety

## USA TODAY Snapshots®

A look at statistics that shape your finances

### Job stress can be satisfying

While most workers are satisfied with their jobs (43% "somewhat," 46% "very"), only one in three say their jobs are low stress:

Very stressful — 24%
Moderately stressful — 43%
Little stressful — 24%
Not stressful — 10%

Note: Exceeds 100% due to rounding

Source: *The Wirthlin Report*          By Cindy Hall and Genevieve Lynn, USA TODAY, 1999

disorder. The point is that because the causes of anxiety disorders are complex, so are the treatments. Treatments are aimed at rebalancing brain chemistry, changing unhealthy beliefs and self-defeating behaviors, and reducing stress through positive lifestyle changes.

# CHAPTER ONE

# PANIC AND FEAR

## CAROL'S STORY

Carol sat in the living room with her parents, discussing the episode she'd had at the mall the day before. It still made her shiver just thinking about it. What could have caused such a reaction? She'd been shopping all day and was hungry and tired. With graduation coming up, she was busy and excited. There was so much to do and think about. They all agreed it was probably just nerves. She needed to relax, eat better, and get some rest.

The next day, Carol drove to the mall by herself. She walked past the place where she'd felt ill. She took a deep breath and felt fine. Then a few days later, while working in the yard, she had another episode. Carol gasped and called out breathlessly. Running from across the yard, her mother found her bent over, gasping for breath. Carol's heart was racing, and she felt dizzy. Her mother helped her to the house and called the doctor. She was feeling better by the time they arrived at the office. All the same, the doctor ran tests over the next several weeks.

During that time, Carol continued to have occasional episodes. The tests came out negative for a physical cause for Carol's symptoms. As the weeks passed, Carol became increasingly fearful of going anywhere alone. What if she had one of the episodes and no one was around to help her? Until now, she had recovered within a few minutes. But what if help wasn't available, she was alone, and she didn't recover so quickly? What if this mysterious illness finally overtook her? She could die alone with no one to help her.

Carol also feared the humiliation of having an episode in public. It was terribly embarrassing. She'd feel the stares of people who wondered *what was wrong, what they could do to help. Carol was sure many people thought she was just trying to draw attention to herself. She confided only in two close friends and made them promise to stay with her as much as possible at school. Twice she had minor episodes in the hall. Her friends took her to the restroom, where she recovered quickly. Many days, she just stayed home, too overwhelmed by the thought of having one of the episodes at school. She rarely went anywhere besides school or doctor visits and only if she was accompanied by one of her parents or friends.*

*Carol's doctor explained to her and her parents that everything looked fine physically. Carol's heart was healthy. Nothing was wrong with her lungs. Her blood work looked fine. He suspected she had panic disorder. Her parents weren't surprised to find out that she had an anxiety disorder. They both had family members with anxiety. The surprising thing was how Carol's panic attacks came on so suddenly, without warning.*

*The doctor explained that this is typical of panic attacks. People with panic disorder seem to have extra-sensitive fight-or-flight systems. After the first panic attack, their bodies and brains become even more alert to threat. The person may not even be aware of the threat. It could be only a very slight rise in heart rate that other people wouldn't notice. The good news was that treatment was available. Carol's doctor referred her to a psychologist, who began treatment with cognitive behavioral therapy.*

## PANIC DISORDER

Panic disorder is a fairly common condition that affects about 2 to 4 percent of people, men and women alike. It consists of two major components. The first is the panic attack, an initial frightening experience of brief but very intense fear that occurs out of the blue.

The second component is an ongoing preoccupation with the fear of having another panic attack in the future. Most people have their first panic attack in their early twenties and very rarely before the age of sixteen or after fifty. For reasons that are not well understood, the number of women with panic disorder outnumbers that of men by a ratio of 2 to 1.

This book bases the criteria for diagnosing each anxiety disorder on the *Diagnostic and Statistical Manual of Mental Disorders IV*, or *DSM-IV*. It was written by a large group of leading experts in the field of psychiatry and mental health and is considered the bible of the field of psychiatry. A person can be considered to have panic disorder if he or she:

- Has recurrent, unexpected, out-of-the-blue panic attacks
- Has at least one of the following for a month or more:
  - Persistent worry about having future attacks
  - Worry about the implications of the attacks (such as "I'm losing control, going crazy, or having a heart attack")
  - A change in behavior due to the attacks (such as avoiding certain places including malls or movie theaters, driving long distances, or other situations for fear of having another panic attack)
  - Has panic attacks that are not due to organic factors (such as taking in too much caffeine) or a general medical condition (such as hyperthyroidism or hypoglycemia)
  - Has panic attacks that are not due to another mental disorder (such as drug abuse)

Panic attacks are sudden waves of severe anxiety that begin abruptly. The symptoms usually last only a few minutes, although they can return in waves for a couple of hours. What does a panic attack feel like? At least four of the following symptoms are present in full-blown panic attacks. (If only two or three are present, it is referred to as a limited-symptom attack.)

- Racing or pounding heart (palpitations)
- Sweating
- Trembling or shaking
- Shortness of breath (dyspnea)
- Feeling of tightness in the throat or choking
- Chest pain or discomfort
- Nausea or abdominal distress
- Feeling dizzy, unsteady, or faint
- Feeling unreal or detached
- Numbness or tingling sensations (paresthesia)
- Chills or hot flashes
- Fear of dying
- Fear of going crazy or losing control

## AGORAPHOBIA

Panic attacks can be terrifying. But even worse is the fear of having another panic attack. Imagine having a panic attack and then living every day in fear of having another one. A person who has panic attacks often becomes intensely focused on avoiding the very physical sensations—rapid heartbeat, sweating, shortness of breath, muscle tension, etc.—that accompanied his or her panic attacks. These sensations are associated with specific situations where escape is difficult or help is either unavailable or will attract the attention of others.

The pattern of avoiding places and situations considered unsafe is called agoraphobia. The word *agoraphobia* comes from Greek words meaning "fear of the marketplace." The panicker views the anticipation of public (marketplace) humiliation and loss of control to be as terrifying as the panic sensations themselves. Agoraphobia affects around 5 percent of the population. About half the people with panic disorder also develop agoraphobia. This is called panic disorder with agoraphobia. Some people develop agoraphobia alone, and this is called agoraphobia without history of panic disorder.

Agoraphobics may feel fear in enclosed areas, crowded places, and open spaces, and while home alone. Areas that cause fear include elevators, tunnels, bridges, stores, open fields, theaters, restaurants, hairsalons, and public transportation vehicles. Often, they occur a certain distance from home or outside the city limits. Agoraphobics also try to avoid situations where there seems to be a high probability of triggering panic sensations. An example is the panicker who fears the sensation of shortness of breath. This person may consistently avoid climbing a flight of stairs, doing strenuous exercise, or being in a crowded room or a shopping mall.

Many agoraphobics feel safe going outside only with a "safe person." This person, often a spouse, a parent, or a close friend, is aware of the agoraphobic's fears and avoidance patterns. The panicker views the safe person as someone who can provide safety during a panic attack. In addition, some panickers feel they must have particular objects such as tranquilizers, cell phones, or bottles of water while out in areas they consider unsafe. The mere thought of going out without one of these safety objects can cause anxiety to spike.

People with agoraphobia often describe their fears as if they have a fear of specific places, such as shopping malls or elevators. Actually, their fear is of the bodily sensations and distressing thoughts that become associated with specific places and situations where these seem most likely to occur and where easy escape may not be available or possible. For this reason, panic disorder and agoraphobia (as well as the other anxiety disorders) have often been described as the "fear of fear."

# WHAT CAUSES PANIC DISORDER AND AGORAPHOBIA?

Why do some people develop panic disorder and agoraphobia? Research points to a genetic predisposition toward being excessively anxious and apprehensive (fearful). For these persons, their fight-or-flight system seems to be extra sensitive, almost out of control at times. The parts of the brain that activate the process, which include the amygdala, the anterior cingulate cortex, and locus coeruleus, get set off without any apparent threat, like an antitheft alarm in a car that gets set off even when no one is near. The brain sends adrenaline racing through the body, causing the heart to beat faster and breathing to speed up.

A person's past experience and history is an important aspect of vulnerability to panic disorder. They determine in part whether a particular physical sensation is interpreted as dangerous or just a bother to be ignored. The most important factor is the family environment in which a person was brought up. Research studies have shown that early experiences with uncontrollable events such as family illness, death, and other traumas may increase vulnerability to developing anxiety disorders, including panic. For example, parents who focus too much on the fear of and prevention of illness in their children may predispose them to overfocus on the dangers of bodily sensations as adults.

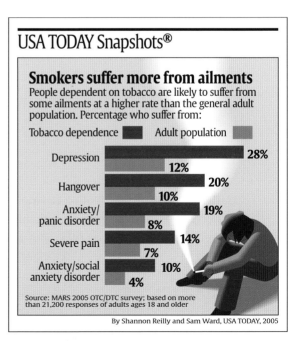

## USA TODAY Snapshots®

### Smokers suffer more from ailments

People dependent on tobacco are likely to suffer from some ailments at a higher rate than the general adult population. Percentage who suffer from:

Tobacco dependence ▮   Adult population ▮

| Ailment | Tobacco dependence | Adult population |
|---|---|---|
| Depression | 28% | 12% |
| Hangover | 20% | 10% |
| Anxiety/panic disorder | 19% | 8% |
| Severe pain | 14% | 7% |
| Anxiety/social anxiety disorder | 10% | 4% |

Source: MARS 2005 OTC/DTC survey; based on more than 21,200 responses of adults ages 18 and older

By Shannon Reilly and Sam Ward, USA TODAY, 2005

**June 26, 2009**

From the Pages of USA TODAY

# Major league anxiety

## *Players more openly seek help for mental pressures*

Khalil Greene endured such agony playing the game he loved, he had to get away from it.

Dontrelle Willis lost control to such an extent, his team put him on the disabled list twice.

[Both] players were on or off the DL [disabled list] because of anxiety-related issues in the last eight days, an unusual confluence that underscores the mental challenges of playing baseball at its highest level.

"This is a source of a lot of joy, but it's also a source of a lot of frustration and sadness and fear," says Greene, an infielder for the St. Louis Cardinals. "It's difficult to deal with, because it is something I really enjoy doing, but it has become at times like a love-hate relationship.

Three years after leaving the team to deal with his social anxiety disorder, Kansas City Royals right-hander Zack Greinke has emerged as one of the majors' best pitchers. Now, in a sport rooted in a macho culture, others have felt compelled to acknowledge the rigors of the game can be too much to bear without help.

"You've dealt with Tommy John surgeries and rotator cuffs so many times that you get used to what the guidelines are," says

Detroit Tigers general manager Dave Dombrowski, whose team has termed Willis's condition an anxiety disorder. "But I've never been involved with a situation like this, so everything you hear and deal with is new."

### Greene's constant battle

Greene had to see a number of doctors and try different treatments until finding the right combination of medication and therapy.

He says he wages a constant, exhausting battle trying to push away negative thoughts and replace them with positive ones. In the last two seasons, that has been more difficult as his performance has declined, feeding into his fear of failure and leading to sudden outbursts.

For the most part, Greene's teammates have given him space while trying to remain supportive.

"I think it would be better to share it, speak with your teammates, because we might be able to help more than he thinks," said two-time MVP Albert Pujols, who has reached out to Greene.

Besides playing for a new team, Greene is finishing a two-year, $11 million contract. That can be one factor that can cause anxiety, according to Greg Dale, the director of sports psychology at Duke University.

Dale, who has counseled college, Olympic and pro athletes, says heightened expectations, fear of failure and attention from the news media also can create anxiety.

"It can become very debilitating to where you begin to almost paralyze yourself and you can't perform something that comes very natural to you," Dale says.

**'Still a great deal of stigma'**
Despite a greater societal awareness of mental health issues, seeking help takes a leap of faith for athletes, says Wes Sime, a sports psychologist who recently retired [from] the University of Nebraska.

"There is still a great deal of stigma," Sime says. "It's reassuring to know more and more are acknowledging it. It's very possible many who have had this in the past have been too afraid to suggest they had something of that nature."

On-field success stories might ease the stigma. With the club's blessing, Greinke left the Royals in spring training 2006 and didn't pitch until June that year, in the minor leagues. This season, he is 9-3, and his 1.90 ERA leads the American League.

"In recent years, (teams) dealt with it in a much more upfront manner," Sime says, "and (have) been more compassionate toward the player, rather than being so macho as in the past, expecting them to suck it up."

**Rougher road for some**
But the path to success is rarely so smooth; in Willis's case, it has been marked by fits and starts.

Willis missed the first six weeks of the season and is disabled again after going 1-4 with a 7.49 ERA in seven starts, during which control problems that initially sidelined him grew worse.

The team doctors' diagnosis of Willis's condition stands at odds with his assessment. The left-hander insists his problems are mechanical and that he feels fine on the mound.

"I don't feel like anything's wrong, other than me playing bad," says Willis, 27. "I feel great. I still have a good time on the field. I still love coming here. As far as people categorizing, they can say whatever they want to. The bottom line is whether you're playing well or not."

[Joey] Votto, the Cincinnati Reds first baseman and top hitter, showed symptoms of distress when he had to leave three games in May.

The team put him on the DL on May 30 with what it called "stress-related issues." Upon returning to the lineup Tuesday, Votto revealed he had been having panic attacks while grieving the loss of his father, who died in August.

Eventually, Votto sought counseling.

Concerned about the stigma of succumbing to stress, he kept his condition private, even from his teammates, until doctors convinced him opening up would be therapeutic.

Sime and Dale think others will come forward as the stigma fades, but the stress inherent to the major leagues remains.

"There are more pressures going on right now, more insecurity about losing position, status," Sime says. "And it just makes players more vulnerable."

*—Jorge L. Ortiz*

Most people report a period of significant life stress preceding their first panic attack. Stressful life events such as family illness, death, job change, a move, or a personal loss can set the process of emotional hyperarousal in motion. This can lead to a panic attack in a vulnerable person. While most people may respond with curiosity or annoyance to a sudden rapid pulse, a vulnerable person may have a panic attack. After the first panic attack, a person will be on high alert, fearing another episode.

## SOCIAL PHOBIA

About 2 to 7 percent of people have social phobia. Also known as social anxiety disorder, or SAD, social phobia is more prevalent in females than in males. The disorder most often starts during those years when social relationships take on immense importance— the adolescent years. People with this disorder experience severe anxiety in social situations. They fear the scrutiny of others, which will make them horribly embarrassed or humiliated. They may also fear that others will think they're stupid, weak, or crazy.

This is far worse than the nervous butterflies most people feel in new social situations such as a first date, meeting new people at a party, or a job interview. Mild to moderate nervousness helps motivate us to try our hardest and to make the best impression we can on others. In social phobia, the fear is intense and interferes significantly with the person's normal routine, school or work functioning, social activities, or relationships. The person also feels great distress about having the anxiety and fear.

For the person with social phobia, many everyday social situations are anxiously anticipated, avoided, or endured only with great discomfort. These include parties, meeting new people, meetings, conversations with strangers, job interviews, talking to authority figures such as teachers, dating, public speaking, performing, participating in sports, eating or drinking in front of other people, using public restrooms, and writing in front of other people. Reactions to social situations can vary from stomach pains, inner anxiety, muscle tension, and dry mouth to stuttering, sweating, and full-blown panic attacks.

Some people feel anxious only in specific situations. Public speaking is the most common form of social phobias. Stage fright is another term frequently used to describe this type of social phobia, especially when it is associated with fear of musical or other artistic performance.

When a person has a fear of a number of social situations, it is sometimes called generalized social anxiety disorder. Although the onset is typically in early adolescence, people often don't seek treatment for social phobia until they are in their thirties. Early treatment is important because people with mild social phobia are at risk for the phobia worsening over time. They are also at risk for developing other anxiety disorders, depression, and alcohol and substance abuse. Social phobia tends to run in families.

People who develop the disorder appear to be born with a genetic vulnerability. Children who are shy and timid are more likely to develop social phobia later. Some patients report that their parents were critical and overprotective.

Some studies demonstrate the differences in the brains of people with and those without social phobia. The most interesting findings to date appeared in a study conducted at Duke University in North Carolina. A team of researchers, including Drs. Jonathan Davidson and Nicholas Potts, compared magnetic resonance imaging (MRI) scans of the brains of patients with social phobia and those of the brains of people without the disorder. They found that a structure in the middle part of the brain, called the putamen, shrank in size more rapidly with age in the patients with social phobia. The putamen produces a neurotransmitter, or chemical messenger, called dopamine. Other

## The Human Brain

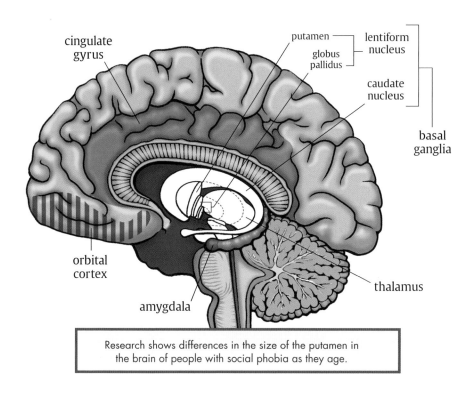

Research shows differences in the size of the putamen in the brain of people with social phobia as they age.

research also indicates an imbalance in the way social phobia patients' brains handle the neurotransmitters dopamine and serotonin. This knowledge will someday help doctors develop more effective treatments for social phobia.

## SPECIFIC PHOBIAS

People with specific phobias have an excessive or unreasonable fear of one particular type of object or situation. They avoid such situations. When they do encounter them, they feel intense fear and anxiety, even panic. Typical specific phobias include fears of snakes, spiders, dogs, cats, flying, heights, water, blood, needles, and dental procedures.

Almost anything can be the object of a phobia. A small sample of the vast range of possible specific phobias includes the following:

- Agrizoophobia—fear of wild animals
- Ailurophobia—fear of cats
- Altophobia—fear of heights
- Coprophobia—fear of feces
- Cynophobia—fear of dogs or rabies
- Dentophobia—fear of dentists
- Electrophobia—fear of electricity
- Emetophobia—fear of vomiting
- Equinophobia—fear of horses
- Hemophobia—fear of blood
- Hydrophobophobia—fear of rabies
- Ichthyophobia—fear of fish
- Triskaidekaphobia—fear of the number 13
- Xenophobia—fear of strangers or foreigners

About 8 percent of people experience phobias. Illness phobias are more common in men, and animal phobias are more common in women. Phobias are caused by a variety of factors. As with other anxiety disorders, it appears that the tendency to develop phobias runs in families. Genetic factors also predispose a person to

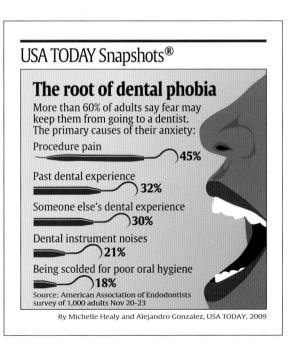

USA TODAY Snapshots®

**The root of dental phobia**

More than 60% of adults say fear may keep them from going to a dentist. The primary causes of their anxiety:

Procedure pain — 45%

Past dental experience — 32%

Someone else's dental experience — 30%

Dental instrument noises — 21%

Being scolded for poor oral hygiene — 18%

Source: American Association of Endodontists survey of 1,000 adults Nov 20-23

By Michelle Healy and Alejandro Gonzalez, USA TODAY, 2009

July 18, 2008

From the Pages of USA TODAY

# Want to ground your fear of flying? Try taking a class

## Airports, airlines can show you that flying is safe

No matter what your pilot tells you, taking a plane trip these days could be irritating, uncomfortable and even maddening.

For millions of people, it also is absolutely frightening.

Despite statistics that show flying is one of the safest modes of travel, many people will only fly if they must. Others are so afraid of flying that they will never travel by air. And when people are too afraid to fly, they can ground not only themselves, but their families, their vacations and their careers.

For years, Maria Smyth, 42, was one of those truly fearful fliers. Smyth, who runs an office-services business out of her Phoenix [Arizona] home, did whatever she could to avoid flying.

"I know planes are safe. I know the statistics. But what I worry about is if something does go wrong, I can't say, 'Let me help you out.' I don't have any control over what's happening."

Smyth's fear made her turn down offers to teach classes in other cities. For years, she put off making plane reservations to visit her grandfather. Then her grandfather died, and "I couldn't even go to his funeral. I decided to take control of my life and not be paralyzed like this anymore."

Fortunately, she found free monthly classes at the Phoenix airport. Taught by Ron Nielsen, a veteran airline pilot with a master's degree in counseling, the Cleared

develop phobias. Some fears may be learned from parents. A young child can develop a phobia by observing a parent with a similar fear. Phobias can also develop after a traumatic event, such as a disaster, an accident, or an illness. Specific phobias may not cause a problem in the person's life until it becomes impossible for the person to continue to avoid the feared situation or object. For example, the fear of

4 Takeoff seminar is similar to various programs around the country.

First, participants are encouraged to identify and talk about what scares them. "We educate people about flying and airplanes," Nielsen says. "We identify the noises and point out that most of them are routine."

Then members learn coping techniques, such as breathing exercises or listening to unfamiliar music or a book on tape.

Every three months, he schedules a session that ends with a short round-trip flight in which class members fly together as a group. Nielsen says it helps fearful fliers "get support from me and their peers."

Twice each year, during October and February, an Overcoming Fear of Flying class is offered by Milwaukee's General Mitchell International Airport [in Wisconsin]. The four-session course costs $175 and includes three classes at the airport and one short round-trip flight with Michael Tomaro, a Milwaukee aviation psychologist and certified flight instructor who has been the course instructor for 20 years.

Tomaro says fear of flying is really a safety question for everyone who flies. "Other passengers may not know how to deal with someone who's having an anxiety attack, and that can raise the anxiety level of everyone in the cabin. And flight crews not trained in how to deal with fearful fliers can mistakenly escalate someone into the throes of a panic attack instead of helping."

Nielsen, with the Cleared 4 Takeoff classes in Phoenix, says that although air travel is definitely becoming more stressful, it's not really the long lines at the airport, the Transportation Security Administration or the threat of terrorism that makes people afraid to fly. Rather, "those are the triggers that release these little time bombs inside people who are already afraid to fly."

Maria Smyth knows all about those triggers. She has taken Nielsen's class several times and now flies once or twice a year. She's by no means a carefree flier. "I still need a little bit of medication to fly and only recently stopped leaving my will out on my dresser each time."

But she has made progress. She and her husband, Phil, flew to Orlando [Florida] for their 10th wedding anniversary. And last May, Smyth flew to Philadelphia [Pennsylvania] to surprise her grandmother for Mother's Day.

"I'm still working on it," Smyth says. "My goal now is to be able to fly like 'normal' people."

—*Harriet Baskas*

heights could overwhelm a person who gets an important job in an office on the twenty-second floor of a tall building.

For those who suffer with anxiety, fear, and panic, help and hope are available. In recent years, doctors have learned a great deal about how to treat anxiety disorders and how to help people handle stress, anxiety, and fear.

# CHAPTER TWO

# RITUALS, TRAUMA, AND WORRY

## JAKE'S STORY

As a boy, Jake had played outside and gotten dirty, just like any other kid. It didn't bother him to have soiled clothes, sticky hands, or dirty fingernails. In school he learned how diseases are transferred. He read about tiny bacteria that can be spread by not washing hands well enough. They said twenty seconds was long enough. But was it really? What if he touched the faucet with his clean hands when he was washing? Or what if he touched the doorknob on the way out of the bathroom? As he thought of all the possibilities, his hand-washing procedure became more elaborate. Sometimes he would lose track of how long he'd been washing, or he'd think maybe he had touched the faucet or the inside of the sink and have to start over again. Then simply thinking a bad thought would make him feel uneasy and he'd have to wash again. Slowly, as the days and months passed, Jake's doubts about cleanliness and safety took up more and more of his time and energy.

Eventually, Jake was consumed with the need to wash his hands—he was washing hands at least one hundred times a day. He showered before school, immediately when he arrived home, and before bed. Each shower lasted at least thirty minutes, each body part washed in a specific order. Sometimes a thought occurred to him or just a bad feeling. Something bad was going to happen to his mother, his brother, or a friend. He'd have to start over with his washing order, and the shower would take even longer. Often the hot water ran out and he shivered, showering with cold water, but he had to finish in the right order.

With all his showering and hand washing, Jake still didn't feel clean. He felt anxious most of the time. The world seemed like a dangerous place, with germs everywhere. He worried about getting a disease, but even more, he worried about spreading a disease. What if he had an illness and spread it to someone else before he even knew he was sick? He'd be responsible. He felt sure he could make a small child or an elderly person sick just by touching them with his "unclean" hands. What if he touched an item and then someone else touched it? He checked on people he'd been in contact with to make sure they were still well.

One day, Jake's dad found him standing at the sink washing his hands over and over. The water was cold, since the hot water had long run out. Jake's hands were red and wrinkled. He stared at his dad and said, "I need help." He hadn't told his parents how worried he was about the germs or harm coming to his family and friends. It all seemed so strange. Even he didn't understand the thoughts that just seemed to pop into his head. He'd also kept secret how often he had been washing his hands. The psychologist they consulted explained that this is not unusual. Jake had obsessive-compulsive disorder.

The intrusive thoughts Jake was having are not thoughts people with the disorder would expect or want to have. They know their compulsions are un-necessary. But they feel a need to do them anyway, so they often keep the symp-toms secret. Jake was re-lieved to find out he wasn't crazy and that there was ef-fective treatment available for his illness.

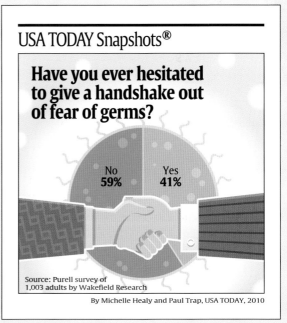

USA TODAY Snapshots®

**Have you ever hesitated to give a handshake out of fear of germs?**

No
59%

Yes
41%

Source: Purell survey of 1,003 adults by Wakefield Research

By Michelle Healy and Paul Trap, USA TODAY, 2010

January 15, 2004

From the Pages of USA TODAY

# Obsessive-compulsive disorder; Early intervention helps. Kids need treatment before rituals are ingrained

## A Better Life; Health, education & science

At age 8, Elyse Monti of East Greenwich, R.I., was staying up half the night to do homework.

In Elyse's mind, it had to be perfect.

"All my obsessions were on school," she says. "Am I doing this right? I'd spend hours on homework. If I couldn't get a math problem, I'd start crying."

Elyse has obsessive-compulsive disorder.

About a third of adults with the disorder say their symptoms began in childhood, but effective treatments for children are not widely known, and therapists familiar with OCD in children are rare.

In Elyse's case, her father was alert to the symptoms because he has OCD himself. Her parents took her to a doctor for evaluation, and she began weekly therapy.

Her symptoms lessened but recur with major life changes. Upon entering high school, "I felt I had so much work to do, I didn't take time to eat. I was out of control," says Elyse, 17. "I couldn't do my homework; I was obsessing. It just keeps going round and round in circles. I just felt this unbelievable high level of anxiety."

Her worried parents sought help, and Elyse was hospitalized in the adolescent unit at Bradley Hospital in East Providence [Rhode Island] for three weeks. To explain her absence from school, she told her friends she had mononucleosis. "You get really good at hiding it," she says. "People with OCD don't want to show it."

Bradley is one of a handful of hospitals at the forefront of researching OCD in children. Child psychiatrist Henrietta Leonard and psychologist Jennifer Freeman, co-directors of the Pediatric Anxiety Research Clinic at Bradley/Hasbro Research Center in Providence [Rhode Island], are leading studies on how to treat OCD in young children.

The researchers have developed a form of cognitive behavioral therapy, CBT, that is being used successfully to help children as young as 5.

The family is "the critical component of the treatment," Leonard says, so "essentially we teach the family to deliver the CBT treatment."

Young patients are encouraged, gently

and over time, to confront whatever it is that they fear.

A child may have washed her hands 30 times in a day but be terrified of leaving the house without washing them once more. In that case, a parent might remind the child of another time when she didn't wash her hands and nothing bad happened, and suggest waiting a few minutes for the fear to pass away.

Often, medications can help. A recent study by researchers at Duke University found that a combination of behavioral therapy and anxiety-reducing drugs is more effective than either approach on its own, says pediatrician Susan Swedo of the National Institute of Mental Health. The medications "allow the child to do internal behavioral therapy and provide stress relief."

But treatment can't begin unless there is a diagnosis. About 15% of children with OCD have a relative who also has it, but "most of it comes out of the blue," Swedo says, and parents may not recognize it.

Early diagnosis is important because therapy is more effective before rituals and obsessions become entrenched, and "there's also a demoralization that comes with having symptoms for a long time."

People with OCD know "what they're experiencing doesn't make any sense," she says. "They are frightened and try to hide it as long as possible. People may spend six or seven hours a day on their rituals, and nobody knows."

Elyse was given help at an early age, but she kept her condition a secret until her sophomore year of high school, when she was assigned to write a personal essay and read it aloud in English class.

"I thought this would be a good time to come out about my OCD," Elyse says. The responses from friends "were all so positive. People said: 'If there's anything I can do,' or 'You were strong to come out about it.'"

Buoyed by that support, Elyse has become an advocate for awareness of OCD in teens and children and is active in the Obsessive-Compulsive Foundation, a national research and support group.

Meanwhile, she's busy at school, where she's an A-student, vice president of the student council and secretary of the student government. She also plays field hockey and runs track. She's looking forward to college next fall.

Her OCD is "not completely gone. It's never gone," she says. "It's cyclical. There's always an event that triggers it. Last year, it was the SATs. That was like the only thing I could think about." Her medication was adjusted for a week, "then the SATs were over, and I was fine. But I know there are still bumps in the road."

[Susan Anderson Swedo] says there is a form of OCD that is associated with a strep infection that affects about one in 10 children with OCD. Called PANDAS (Pediatric Autoimmune Neuropsychiatric Disorder Associated with Streptococcal infections), it is marked by sudden onset of symptoms. "Most OCD starts gradually," Swedo says, but with PANDAS, it can develop in hours. If treated promptly with antibiotics, she says, symptoms can in many cases disappear in days.

—*Anita Manning*

# OBSESSIVE-COMPULSIVE DISORDER

One out of forty people has obsessive-compulsive disorder, or about 2.5 percent of the U.S. population. It usually begins before the age of thirty, in childhood or adolescence, but can also have a later onset. People with OCD experience persistent thoughts, impulses, ideas, or images. While most of us can dismiss these fairly easily, people with OCD can't ignore them. The ideas and images cause such intense anxiety and distress that people with OCD feel they must do something to get relief.

Compulsions, or rituals, develop in an effort to relieve the distress and anxiety brought on by obsessions. These compulsions are repetitive behaviors that can include checking, cleaning, hand washing, repeating actions, and ordering. They can also be repetitive mental acts such as praying, counting, repeating words silently, and going over events in one's mind.

Compulsions are often done with a vague goal of magically preventing or avoiding a dreaded event, death, or illness. There may or may not be a relationship between the compulsion and the dreaded event. A person might check the arrangement of books on a shelf as a response to an obsessive thought about harm coming to a loved one, for example. Obsessive-compulsive disorder manifests itself in a variety of ways. Checking, washing, and cleaning compulsions are the most common, but there are many other types of compulsions.

People with checking compulsions have irrational fears of terrible things happening to themselves or others as a result of things they do or do not do. They may check door locks or household appliances or check their homework and test questions repeatedly. Those with washing and cleaning compulsions wash their hands, shower, or clean their surroundings to ease excessive fears or worries about contamination by germs, dirt, or foreign substances. Others arrange certain items in exact, or perfect, ways. Books or papers might be kept in a particular order. Some people repeat behaviors in a specific order or insist on things such as shoelaces or socks being perfectly even. For a few people with OCD, their compulsion is to hoard or collect seemingly useless items.

Other people with OCD have obsessive thoughts that center on religious and moral issues. This form of OCD, called scrupulosity, has been observed in the writings of such famous historical religious figures as Martin Luther and Saint Ignatius Loyola, who lived about five hundred years ago. Some people with OCD don't appear to have compulsions, but in fact, they have mental compulsions. They have primarily obsessional OCD and are troubled by unwanted, intrusive, horrific thoughts and images of causing danger or harm to others. Examples include unwanted, violent thoughts to harm loved ones or engaging in some morally unacceptable behavior, such as an embarrassing sexual act.

To ease the distress caused by the obsessive thoughts, many people with OCD purposefully engage in repetitive thoughts, such

Some people with OCD compulsively hoard things. They are unable to throw anything away, and their homes fill with trash. Throwing away or thinking about discarding items can lead to feelings of anxiety.

as praying, counting, or repeating certain words. They may also mentally review distressing situations to reassure themselves. The compulsive thoughts and mental reviews help at first but soon prove inadequate to relieve the anxiety. Cycles of obsessive and compulsive thoughts take up increasing amounts of time, often reaching almost every waking hour. And despite the power and distress of the thoughts, it is the hallmark of the disorder that the person with OCD never actually acts upon the thoughts.

Whatever the compulsions—checking, washing, ordering, or praying—performing them once won't be enough. The list of things to be checked or washed grows, because relief is only temporary. The anxiety and distress return, and more compulsions are needed. Of course, most of us have had some obsessive thoughts. And haven't we all checked and rechecked a test paper or checked to make sure the door was locked or a candle was blown out? Only when obsessive-compulsive behavior significantly interferes with daily living, with functioning at home, school, or work and when it causes a great deal of distress is the condition likely to be diagnosed as OCD.

OCD tends to run in families, so there appears to be a genetic predisposition. An imbalance in the neurotransmitter serotonin plays a role in OCD. Brain imaging studies have shown abnormalities in several parts of

## Why the body may 'choke'

Excessive activity in the anterior cingulate gyrus (the middle part of the brain) has been associated with mental blocks and other obsessive behavior, causing people to "think too much."

White indicates the most active areas of the brain. In this case it pinpoints overactivity in the anterior cingulate gyrus, the brain's gear shifter.

**Cingulate gyrus**
Within the frontal lobes

**Cerebellum**

**Healthy image:** Shows good, full, symmetrical activity in the front tip of the brain called the prefrontal cortex, the brain's internal monitor or supervisor.

**Abnormal image:** Identifies decreased activity in the prefrontal cortex, which can cause people to lose focus and have problems with impulse control.

Source: Amen Clinic for Behavioral Medicine, Fairfield, Calif.    By Bob Laird and Frank Pompa, USA TODAY, 2000

the brains of people with OCD, including the orbital cortex, thalamus, basal ganglia, caudate nucleus, and cingulate gyrus.

Occasionally, OCD can develop suddenly in children who develop strep throat. The body appears to form antibodies against the streptococci bacteria, which then attack certain structures within the brain. This leads to OCD symptoms or worsening of existing OCD symptoms. This reaction to strep is called Pediatric Autoimmune Neuropsychiatric Disorders Associated with Streptococcal Infections, or PANDAS. When treatment with traditional antibiotic medications to kill off the strep bacteria is begun, the symptoms of PANDAS rapidly decline.

## POST-TRAUMATIC STRESS DISORDER

The symptoms of post-traumatic stress disorder (PTSD) have been described in the psychiatric literature since World War I (1914–1918). Soldiers coming back from the war were said to have shell shock, soldier's heart, or war neurosis. They had anxiety, nightmares, and flashbacks for weeks, months, or years after coming back from fighting the war. Psychiatrists later saw the similarities between the symptoms soldiers experienced and those of people who had experienced other devastating traumatic events such as accidents and natural disasters.

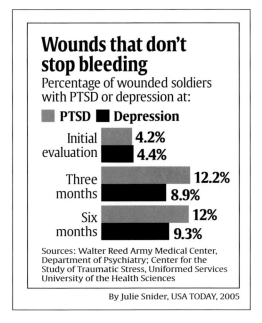

**Wounds that don't stop bleeding**

Percentage of wounded soldiers with PTSD or depression at:

■ **PTSD** ■ **Depression**

Initial evaluation
**4.2%**
**4.4%**

Three months
**12.2%**
**8.9%**

Six months
**12%**
**9.3%**

Sources: Walter Reed Army Medical Center, Department of Psychiatry; Center for the Study of Traumatic Stress, Uniformed Services University of the Health Sciences

By Julie Snider, USA TODAY, 2005

October 27, 2008

From the Pages of USA TODAY

# Post-traumatic stress is a war within the body

## But military combat is not the top cause of biological condition

Post-traumatic stress disorder (PTSD), once a poorly understood and little-known mental health problem, is turning up on the public's radar a lot more as growing numbers of Iraq and Afghanistan war veterans seek treatment for the illness.

About one out of seven service members have returned from deployments with symptoms of the disorder, according to a Rand Corp. study out in April. The Department of Veterans Affairs reported about a 70% jump in veterans seeking treatment for PTSD in the 12 months before June 2007 and an additional 50% rise in the next nine months.

Despite all the public attention, myths about PTSD abound, says Farris Tuma, chief of the traumatic stress program at the National Institute of Mental Health.

One myth is that the disorder is only psychological. But it's a biologically based condition, says Tuma, with the body's stress-response system in overdrive.

Possibly the most widespread myth is that the top cause of PTSD is military combat. Research says it's auto accidents.

Treatment gives most people relief from symptoms, Tuma says. Specialized therapies and/or medication, usually SSRI [selective serotonin reuptake inhibitor] antidepressants such as Zoloft, work best, he adds. But Americans with PTSD wait an average of 12 years before getting treated.

Although many shrug off symptoms on their own or with the help of friends, the disorder can linger for others. About 20% of those in car accidents that caused injuries have PTSD a year after the accident, suggests a long-term study in Albany, N.Y. There were 2.5 million people injured in car crashes last year, according to the National Highway Traffic Safety Administration, so many are at risk.

Lisa Hardimon, 43, feels she was headed toward chronic PTSD after a crash at an intersection rolled her car three times into oncoming traffic, leaving her trapped upside-down under the collapsed roof. A Redondo Beach, Calif., physical therapist and graduate student, she had medical care after the accident, which was seven years ago.

Hardimon's voice breaks and she cries as she describes the worst after-effects: "Getting back in a car was just awful—my heart raced at intersections. I would see like a video of the scene all the time. I couldn't concentrate and had trouble sleeping." A psychologist told her she had PTSD.

The symptoms eased. "It took about a year, though, and it was a conscious decision that I couldn't live this way. I was married and wanted to have kids. . . . I began to block it out, not let myself think about it."

Because PTSD can impair so much of a person's life, mental health experts are concerned about the fallout for young soldiers.

Vietnam veterans with PTSD but no heart disease in their mid-30s were twice as likely as veterans without PTSD to die of heart disease by their 50s, shows a new study by psychologist Joseph Boscarino of the Geisinger Health System in Danville, Pa. That's equal to the greater heart attack risk from smoking two to three packs of cigarettes a day for more than 20 years, Boscarino says.

Although the military screens today's troops for PTSD, which wasn't done during the Vietnam War [1957–1975], about half of recent veterans with PTSD symptoms haven't sought treatment, according to the Rand study this year.

The longer someone has PTSD, the more likely he'll develop drug or alcohol abuse, Tuma says. And sexual problems in veterans with traumatic stress are another concern, says Suzie Chen, who counsels veterans at the VA Hospital in Long Beach, Calif.

Between 63% and 80% of combat veterans with PTSD have sexual problems, according to studies from the Vietnam era through the Iraq war (2003–present). The causes may be biological or emotional. Some don't even sleep in the same rooms as their spouses because of nightmares, she says.

The Pentagon [headquarters of the U.S. armed forces] funneled an unprecedented $300 million this year into new research on PTSD and brain injury.

Symptoms of PTSD:
- Nightmares
- Insomnia
- Flashbacks of frightening event
- Avoiding scenes that remind one of it
- Startling easily
- Trouble concentrating
- Emotional numbness
- Irritability
- Aggression

*Source: National Center for Post-Traumatic Stress Disorder*

For more information on PTSD, visit these websites
- www.ncptsd.va.gov (National Center for PTSD, United States Department of Veterans Affairs)
- centerforthestudyoftraumaticstress. org (Center for the Study of Traumatic Stress)
- adaa.org (Anxiety Disorders Association of America)
- nami.org/veterans (National Alliance on Mental Illness, Veterans Resource Center)

*—Marilyn Elias*

A variety of traumatic events can lead to PTSD, including trauma in battle. This army infantry scout lives with PTSD as a result of military missions in Iraq in the early 2000s.

From this came the notion of a specific psychiatric syndrome originating in the experience of severe trauma. Since PTSD was first established as a diagnosis in 1980, it's been recognized that sexual, physical, and emotional abuse; rape; assault; and even witnessing disasters or death are events that can lead to PTSD symptoms.

The symptoms of PTSD most often occur immediately after a trauma but occasionally surface years later when a person is under further stress. For a person to be diagnosed with PTSD, the following need to be present for at least one month, and they must cause significant distress or impairment. If symptoms last for less than a month, the condition is classified as acute stress disorder.

- Exposure to a traumatic event in which both of the following were present:
  - The person experienced, witnessed, or was confronted with an event(s) that involved actual or threatened death, serious injury, or threat to the physical integrity of self or others.
  - The response involved intense fear, helplessness, or horror.
- Persistent reexperiencing of a traumatic event in one (or more) of the following ways:
  - Recurrent and intrusive distressing recollections
  - Recurrent distressing dreams of the event
  - Acting or feeling as if the traumatic event were occurring again
  - Intense psychological distress at exposure to cues that symbolize or resemble an aspect of the event
  - Physiological reactivity on exposure to cues that symbolize or resemble an aspect of the event
- Avoidance of stimuli associated with the trauma and numbing of general responsiveness, as indicated by three or more of the following:
  - Avoidance of thoughts, feelings, or conversations associated with the trauma
  - Avoidance of activities, places, or people that arouse recollections of the trauma
  - Inability to recall an important aspect of the trauma
  - Markedly diminished interest or participation in significant activities
  - Feeling of detachment or estrangement from others
  - Restricted range of affect (unable to have loving feelings)
  - Sense of foreshortened future (does not expect to have a career, marriage, children, or a normal life span)

- Symptoms of increased arousal (not present before the trauma) as indicated by two or more of the following:
  —Difficulty falling or staying asleep
  —Irritability or outbursts of anger
  —Difficulty concentrating
  —Hypervigilance
  —Exaggerated startle response

Post-traumatic stress disorder affects almost 3.6 percent of Americans. People with PTSD tend to have a higher prevalence of depression, panic disorder, generalized anxiety disorder, social phobia, substance abuse, and suicidal tendencies.

Many people experience horrendous traumatic events and don't develop PTSD. It appears that many factors, environmental and genetic, predict one's vulnerability to PTSD symptoms. In addition to experiencing the traumatic event, genetic makeup, predisposing childhood events, previous traumas, unavailability of social support, and limited coping skills can leave a person more vulnerable to PTSD.

## GENERALIZED ANXIETY DISORDER

About 3.4 percent of Americans have generalized anxiety disorder (GAD). The hallmark of GAD is worry—frequent, uncontrollable worry about negative events that either won't happen soon or have little chance of happening. People with GAD are anxious and worry excessively more days than not. For a person to be diagnosed with GAD, the anxiety and worry must last at least six months, and the person must worry about a number of events and activities, not just a few. In addition to anxiety and worry, people with GAD can feel restless, keyed up, on edge, fatigued, or irritable. They can also have difficulty concentrating, muscle tension, and sleep disturbances. To meet the criteria for a diagnosis of GAD, the anxiety and worry must cause significant distress or impairment and cannot be caused by a medical condition, substance abuse, or any other mental disorder. We all worry. But there is a difference between normal worry and the worry of GAD.

## NORMAL WORRY

- Is focused on only a few future threats
- Helps a person prepare for coping with a future threat. It promotes healthy problem solving to deal with the threat.
- Is in proportion to the real threat being faced
- Is rarely incapacitating or disabling

## GAD WORRY

- Is focused on many diverse and diffuse future threats. The person is worried about everything.
- Involves little effective problem solving. In fact, it may actually interfere with current problem solving. By worrying, the person may feel a false sense of control.
- Is about no distinct threat. It is focused on future events that have little or no realistic chance of happening. It's the "What if . . . ?" disease.
- Involves incapacitating anxiety. It's really out of control.

Generalized anxiety disorder tends to be persistent and chronic. Up to 90 percent of people with the disorder have another psychiatric disorder. Many also have physical symptoms that stem from chronic anxiety, such as headaches, irritable bowel syndrome, and stomach distress. They make many more trips to the doctor than the average person without GAD.

Generalized anxiety disorder appears to run in families. Twin studies indicate at least part of the cause is genetic, but it's apparent that environment also plays a major role. Loss of or separation from

## Advice for Worriers

Two great figures of the twentieth century gave advice on handling worry, fear, and the inevitable traumas, suffering, and dilemmas we all experience from time to time:

When I look back on all these worries, I remember the story of the old man who said on his deathbed that he had had a lot of trouble in his life, most of which had never happened.

—Winston Churchill, prime minister of the United Kingdom,
*Memoirs of the Second World War* (1959)

The encouraging thing is that every time you meet a situation, though you may think at the time it is an impossibility and you go through the tortures of the damned, once you have met it and lived through it you find that forever after you are freer than you ever were before. If you can live through that you can live through anything. You gain strength, courage, and confidence by every experience in which you stop to look fear in the face.

You are able to say to yourself, 'I lived through this horror. I can take the next thing that comes along.'

—Eleanor Roosevelt, wife of President Franklin D. Roosevelt,
*You Learn by Living* (1960)

a parent in early childhood or excessive parental expectations can predispose a person to GAD. Stressful or traumatic events can make a person even more vulnerable.

People with GAD frequently have an imbalance of three neurotransmitters—serotonin, noradrenaline, and GABA (gamma-aminobutyric acid). GABA is a neurotransmitter that works to naturally calm us by toning down brain activity. Medications that affect these neurotransmitters are useful in the treatment of GAD.

Learning new ways to manage stress, relax, worry less, and handle stress-provoking thoughts are also important to long-term relief of anxiety and worry.

# CHAPTER THREE

# TREATMENT OPTIONS

## PAUL'S STORY

Waking from a sound sleep, Paul felt his dog, King, licking his face and heard him barking. He petted his soft fur and told him to be quiet. Then Paul smelled smoke and jumped from his bed. He rushed into the hall with King, banged on his father's and sisters' doors, and yelled for them to get up and out of the house. Frantically, he ran into his brothers' room and grabbed both of them. He carried one and led the other out of the house to safety. He met his sister Dawn on the lawn. She was crying hysterically. Where were Dad and Sharon, their other sister? They hadn't come out yet. Sharon had tripped, and their father had stopped to help her but had demanded that Dawn keep running. Paul rushed back to the house, pushing his way past firefighters, who said it was too dangerous to go back in. He saw his father, unconscious, just inside the doorway. He hadn't been able to reach Sharon either. Paul yelled, and the firefighters came running back in. He passed out, and the firefighters dragged Paul and his father to safety.

Paul spent the next month in the hospital. He had difficulty breathing because of the smoke he had inhaled. Dressing changes for the burns on his arms and legs were agonizing. Even worse was knowing that his little brothers were enduring similar pain. Their burns weren't as severe, but he hated to think of his brothers having to deal with them. His father's burns were even worse, and he was having problems with his breathing. Paul's mother had been out of town caring for her sick mother the night of the fire. She came home right away and was staying with Paul's sister in an apartment near the hospital. Family members, friends, and people they didn't even know helped financially and with household duties and meals. In the newspapers and on the TV news, Paul and his dog were treated like celebrities. Paul had daily interviews, even while he was in the hospital. Once he was home, the town council became involved and gave him a special certificate of commendation. The family's vet treated King's burned paws for free, and a local pet store gave him free pet supplies for life.

To Paul, all the congratulations seemed meaningless and out of place. His sister Sharon had died, and his brothers and father had suffered a great deal from their burns. If only he had smelled the smoke sooner. If only the smoke detector had been working properly. He should have checked it. When people brought up the fire or tried to treat him like a hero, Paul changed the subject. He shrugged off words of admiration, feeling that he didn't deserve them. He didn't remember much about the fire anyway, so he said there wasn't much to talk about. Still, his parents didn't think it was healthy for him to keep his feelings inside. Paul became visibly anxious whenever anyone brought up the fire. He was also super-vigilant about fire prevention. He tested the smoke detector daily and checked stoves and appliances before he went to bed each night.

During the day, Paul was bothered by sudden recollections of his sister Dawn standing on the lawn crying hysterically. Other times he saw an image in his mind of his father and sister Sharon. He'd stretch out his hands but could never reach them. These memories were distressing, because he both wanted to and was afraid to remember the details of the fire.

At night, Paul awoke with nightmares about the fire. His mind seemed to be recalling at night what he couldn't remember during the day. He'd wake up screaming, and someone would run into the room. It embarrassed him when his sister or brothers saw him this way. He felt humiliated and weak. He began to stay up late reading and doing homework, willing himself to stay awake and avoid the horrible

dreams and fears. He found it hard to concentrate though, and his grades began to fall. During the day, he was tired, and he withdrew from outside activities.

Paul's father was also having difficulty dealing with the aftereffects of the fire. He had been having recollections of his experiences as a soldier in Iraq and was having nightmares and flashbacks (sudden memories) of his war experiences and of the fire. He was receiving disability payments due to his injuries from the fire. The family was doing well on that income and on his wife's salary. But the fact that he wasn't working, made him feel useless. He realized he and his son both needed help. He discussed it with Paul, and they sought counseling together. The counselor listened intently to their sad, painful tale and the ways in which the events of that day had dramatically changed their family's lives. Paul and his father learned that they both had symptoms of post-traumatic stress disorder.

## GETTING HELP

Anxiety disorders affect people on physical, mental, emotional, and behavioral levels. The first step toward recovery is a diagnosis by a qualified mental health professional. Preferably this person would be a psychiatrist or a psychologist who specializes in the treatment of anxiety disorders. In the initial sessions, the doctor typically gathers data on the history of the presenting problem and the current symptoms and takes a detailed medical and psychiatric history. Often the patient fills out questionnaires that objectively assess the severity of the presenting problem. A therapist then reviews all this information and comes up with a well-rounded treatment plan to address the patient's needs.

How does a person find a qualified mental health professional? Most people begin by making an appointment with their family

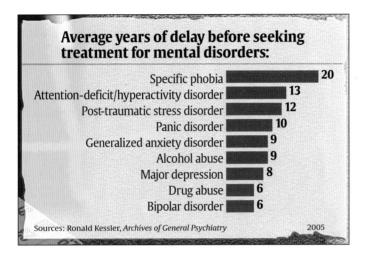

**Average years of delay before seeking treatment for mental disorders:**

|  |  |
|---|---|
| Specific phobia | 20 |
| Attention-deficit/hyperactivity disorder | 13 |
| Post-traumatic stress disorder | 12 |
| Panic disorder | 10 |
| Generalized anxiety disorder | 9 |
| Alcohol abuse | 9 |
| Major depression | 8 |
| Drug abuse | 6 |
| Bipolar disorder | 6 |

Sources: Ronald Kessler, *Archives of General Psychiatry*          2005

doctor, a school counselor, or a mental health clinic. Any trusted health professional in your community can direct you to a qualified mental health professional who can help. However, no matter from whom you seek help, it is important that the person has the background, experience, and success in the treatment of anxiety disorders. By contacting a national organization such as the Anxiety Disorders Association of America (ADAA), the Association for Behavioral and Cognitive Therapies (ABCT), the International OCD Foundation (IOCDF), or the Obsessive-Compulsive Information Center, you can get the names of doctors and therapists who have identified themselves as professionals in treating anxiety disorders. The contact information for these organizations is listed in the Resources section of this book. The organizations don't always track the treatment practices of these professionals, however. Being on a list does not necessarily mean that a professional is competent to treat anxiety disorders, only that he or she has indicated an expertise or interest in the treatment of one or more anxiety disorders.

With names in hand, you can check on a clinician's license and its status by calling your state government's general information

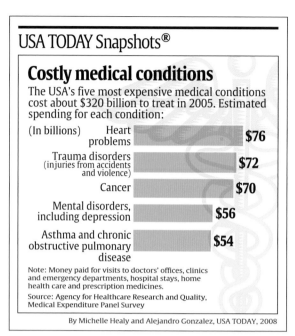

USA TODAY Snapshots®

**Costly medical conditions**

The USA's five most expensive medical conditions cost about $320 billion to treat in 2005. Estimated spending for each condition:

(In billions)

Heart problems — $76

Trauma disorders (injuries from accidents and violence) — $72

Cancer — $70

Mental disorders, including depression — $56

Asthma and chronic obstructive pulmonary disease — $54

Note: Money paid for visits to doctors' offices, clinics and emergency departments, hospital stays, home health care and prescription medicines.

Source: Agency for Healthcare Research and Quality, Medical Expenditure Panel Survey

By Michelle Healy and Alejandro Gonzalez, USA TODAY, 2008

number and asking for the licensing board for that clinician's profession (medicine, psychology, social work, etc.). In this way, you can find information about any disciplinary action that might have been taken against the clinician. If there has been disciplinary action, you might want to consider going to a different clinician.

It's important to realize that a psychiatrist may be needed if medication is part of the treatment plan. Psychiatrists are medical doctors who can prescribe medication. However, they often are not trained to provide cognitive behavioral therapy (CBT), which can be very helpful in treating anxiety disorders. Some have sought this additional training, and many are partnered with psychologists or clinical social workers who do provide CBT. If not, it's imperative that the psychiatrist be willing to make a referral to someone who can provide CBT. Often just seeking help and discovering that there are effective treatments for anxiety disorders brings about a great deal of relief.

## THE BRAIN AND ANXIETY

Your brain is an incredibly intricate system of interconnected nerve cells, or neurons (you're born with 100 billion of them!), that are chained to one another. These connected neurons form circuits that transmit messages in chemical form to all parts of your body. These messages enable the regulation of life-sustaining biological processes, which include the use of our five senses and the functions of digestion, circulation, and respiration among many others. Thinking, feeling, and behaving are also functions of this amazing system of interconnected circuits.

Neurotransmitters are brain chemicals that enable messages to be carried back and forth along these circuits. They bridge synapses—the tiny gaps between nerve cells. Imbalances in the levels of these neurotransmitters can severely disrupt the brain's regulation of the biological processes. The imbalances can disrupt the circuits and the flow of the chemical messages from one neuron to another. The result can be psychiatric disorders, including anxiety disorders.

Three neurotransmitters appear to play major roles in anxiety disorders: serotonin, norepinephrine, and GABA. Norepinephrine can activate the fight-or-flight response, while GABA and serotonin have a calming effect. Serotonin is vital to the brain's capacity to properly regulate moods. People with anxiety disorders can have imbalances of these neurotransmitters. Certain medications correct these imbalances, thereby reducing the person's anxiety symptoms.

## MEDICATIONS

Antidepressants, a group of medications to treat depression, have been found to be highly effective in the treatment of anxiety disorders. These medications are from a family of medications called selective serotonin reuptake inhibitors, or SSRIs. Doctors commonly recommend and prescribe SSRIs such as fluoxetine (Prozac), fluvoxamine (Luvox), paroxetine (Paxil), sertraline (Zoloft), citalopram (Celexa), venlafaxine (Effexor), and escitalopram oxalate (Lexapro). They work for people

with anxiety disorders by increasing the amount of serotonin at the brain's synapses. The chemical bridges the gaps between nerve cells so that chemical messages can flow more effectively. The result is a significant reduction in anxiety symptoms.

Patients generally tolerate these medications and receive the added advantage of reducing depression. The medications are non-habit forming, less sedating, and have far fewer side effects than older antianxiety medications. All SSRIs work in similar ways, but each is somewhat different. Depending on the disorder, SSRIs may take four to eight weeks to achieve a positive result. At times, the first medication a patient uses won't relieve anxiety well enough. A doctor will then prescribe another one. Sometimes a patient will need to try several before finding one that works well. Occasionally, other medications are prescribed along with SSRIs to help relieve anxiety.

Since many anxiety disorders are affected by the neurotrans-mitter GABA, doctors sometimes prescribe medications that affect GABA. These drugs are called benzodiazepines. The ones doctors most commonly recommend are alprazolam (Xanax), clonazepam (Klonopin), diazepam (Valium), and lorazepam (Ativan). Benzodi-azepines work quickly, so patients sometimes take them until the SSRI achieves its full benefit. They are, however, habit forming, and special care must be taken when stopping these medications. Abrupt withdrawal can produce panic attacks, confusion, severe anxiety, muscle tension, irritability, insomnia, and seizures.

Benzodiazepines are most appropriate for short-term treatment. Other antidepressants are also used to treat anxiety disorders, especially in the few cases when SSRIs are not effective. For example, another class of medications, called beta-blockers, can be helpful for reducing the physical symptoms of anxiety, such as rapid or irregular heartbeats, sweating, shaking, and tremors. The two that doctors most commonly prescribe are atenolol (Tenormin) and propranolol

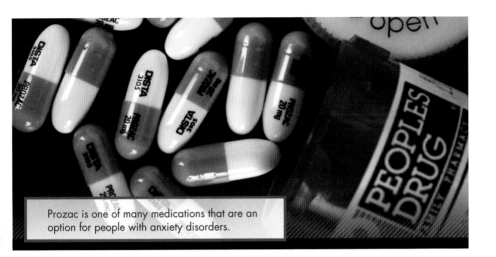

Prozac is one of many medications that are an option for people with anxiety disorders.

(Inderal). They have been used effectively to reduce the symptoms associated with stage fright (the fear of musical or other artistic performance), a common social phobia.

Medication can be an important part of the treatment of an anxiety disorder. However, it should be considered only as partial treatment. Medications alone rarely result in the elimination of all symptoms. A well-rounded treatment plan should include medication plus cognitive behavioral therapy. People with mild or moderate anxiety disorders may even be effectively treated without medication.

## ARE MEDICATIONS FOR ANXIETY DISORDERS SAFE?

In October 2004, the United States Food and Drug Administration (FDA) issued a warning that SSRIs may increase suicidal ideation (thinking) and suicidal behaviors in a small number of children and adolescents. The FDA report was based on a review of twenty-four different short-term studies (four to sixteen weeks) of nine antidepressant medications (SSRIs and others). The studies involved more than forty-four hundred children and adolescents with major depressive disorder, obsessive-compulsive disorder, and other psychiatric disorders. Analyses of the studies showed that, on average, the risk of suicidal

ideation and suicidal behaviors was 4 percent of patients treated with an antidepressant, compared to 2 percent of patients who were given a placebo (sugar pill). In none of the studies did an actual suicide occur.

So while the risks of taking SSRIs are extremely small, doctors and caregivers have increased their monitoring of children taking these medications by looking for changes in behavior. These changes include agitation, restlessness, irritability, or other changes in a child's behavior or personality. Parents should contact their child's doctor if any of these symptoms or other concerns arise. The medication dose may need to be lowered, or the medication may need to be discontinued. Patients should never just stop taking their medication abruptly without their doctor's supervision since this may worsen symptoms.

Monitoring of the patient's response to medication should occur throughout treatment. It should be noted that the FDA warning did not prohibit the use of these medications in children and adolescents. For the vast majority of children with anxiety disorders, these medications are safe and effective. The FDA warning alerts patients and families to the risk of suicidal thoughts and behavior. But the FDA also notes that this risk must be balanced with the clinical need for the medications for each individual child.

## COGNITIVE BEHAVIORIAL THERAPY

In addition to medication, specific types of counseling and psychotherapy have proven to be effective components of successful anxiety treatment. Cognitive behavioral therapy is one such approach. It differs from traditional talk therapies in important ways. Traditional talk therapies focus on the events from the past that may have contributed to the present symptoms. In CBT the focus of treatment is on the present—identifying and changing unhealthy thought patterns and behaviors that currently contribute to the anxiety symptoms.

In addition, due to its focus on the present, CBT tends to be briefer and more effective than talk therapies that focus mostly on the past. Cognitive behavioral therapy is the combination of two treatment approaches—cognitive therapy and behavior therapy. Cognitive therapy uses strategies that help people change the dysfunctional, unhealthy thinking patterns and beliefs behind the symptoms. By actively challenging dysfunctional automatic beliefs, the cognitive therapist helps people change troublesome thinking patterns. The therapist also helps people develop healthier patterns.

Behavior therapy uses strategies that help people change the behavioral patterns that maintain and worsen anxiety symptoms. Especially important in the treatment of anxiety disorders are the exposure-based strategies below.

## COGNITIVE STRATEGIES

According to the principles of cognitive behavioral therapy, our world is shaped not by the events or facts of our lives and the world we live in. Instead, our world is shaped by our appraisals of or our beliefs about ourselves and the world we live in. People with anxiety disorders tend to hold beliefs about themselves and the world based on an unrealistic, often irrationally high expectation of the occurrence of negative, even catastrophic, events. They have persistent feelings of doubt regarding their own or others' personal safety. They have negative thoughts that often begin with, "What if . . ." or "I should have. . . ." Some examples are these:

- "What if I'm having a heart attack?"
- "What if the airplane crashes?"
- "What if I get AIDS?"
- "What if I have a panic attack?"
- "What if I act upon this thought of harming my children?"
- "What if I look stupid, blush, or sweat?"

## Anxiety Disorders and Depression

Many people with OCD and other anxiety disorders suffer from some degree of depressive symptoms. These range from mild (the blues) to severe, life-threatening depressive illness characterized by strong, persistent feelings of sadness, hopelessness, helplessness, loss of interest in normal activities and pursuits, lack of energy, impaired sleep and appetite, and suicidal thoughts. If anxiety is an issue for you, just as Dr. Bruce Hyman advises people with obsessive-compulsive disorder in *The OCD Workbook*, be on the lookout for the warning signs of major clinical depression, since those with major depression often lack the perspective to see what's happening to them. Doctors and family members should watch for warning signs of major clinical depression. The presence of major clinical depression complicates the treatment of anxiety disorders.

The diagnosis of depression is best made by a licensed mental health professional, who may use a variety of clinical tools to assess the likelihood and severity of depression. To help you determine whether you may be depressed and should consult with a mental health professional, we've provided a couple of assessments. The first is a list of the signs of major clinical depression. Check off all that apply to you (or write them on a separate sheet of paper):

Negative thoughts that cause anxiety are almost instantaneous and are often irrational. That's why some therapists refer to them as automatic thoughts. Behind the automatic, often painful and self-

- Depressed mood most of the day, nearly every day
- Diminished interest or pleasure in all or almost all activities
- Significant weight loss or gain, or decrease or increase in appetite nearly every day
- Insomnia or excessive sleep nearly every day
- Feelings of extreme restlessness or being slowed down
- Fatigue or loss of energy nearly every day
- Feelings of worthlessness or excessive or inappropriate guilt nearly every day
- Diminished ability to think or concentrate, or indecisiveness, nearly every day
- Recurrent thoughts of death or of suicide (without a specific plan), or a plan for committing suicide or an actual attempt

The diagnosis of major clinical depression requires that you have at least five of the symptoms above, that they are present for two weeks, and that you experience a noticeable/obvious change in your previous functioning. In addition, one of the symptoms must be either depressed mood or diminished interest or pleasure in activities.

(Adapted from *The OCD Workbook, 3rd ed.*, 2010, by Bruce Hyman, Ph.D., and Cherry Pedrick, R.N.)

torturing thoughts are faulty beliefs about self, others, and the world.

Cognitive strategies focus on discovering these faulty beliefs and then directly challenging and testing them. When we challenge our

automatic beliefs, we find that many of them hold no truth. Once a person has challenged the faulty beliefs and the negative thoughts they breed, he or she can begin to replace them with more positive coping self-statements. This process, over time, enables people to gain more and more control over automatic thoughts.

Keep in mind that challenging faulty beliefs is more than just positive thinking or putting an artificially rosy face on our fear-provoking experiences. It's better to view it more as accurate thinking. Through the process of therapy, dysfunctional, inappropriate beliefs and thoughts are tested, challenged, and replaced with more accurate and functional beliefs and thoughts. Here are some faulty beliefs that are common among people with anxiety disorders:

- All-or-nothing thinking (black-and-white thinking)—"I'm a complete failure because I scored poorly on one test."
- Overgeneralization (isolated negative events applied to all future events)—"She wouldn't go out with me. No one ever will!"
- Mental filter (focusing on one negative detail)—"My vacation was completely ruined because our rental car ran out of gas."
- Mind reading (assuming others' negative opinions)—"My boss must think I'm incompetent. He thinks I'm boring."
- Fortune-teller error/probability overestimation (predicting the future)—"I'll panic." "I'll freeze." "I'll definitely get sick and die."
- Catastrophizing (assuming the worst)—"I have a headache. It certainly means I have cancer."
- Emotional reasoning (feelings are the only evidence)—"I feel it is so, therefore, it must be true." "I feel so foolish and stupid. I must really look foolish and stupid."
- "Should" statements (unreasonably high standards)—"I should always be perfect, say the right thing, and be in perfect control all the time."

**April 2, 2007**

From the Pages of USA TODAY

# Check it out

What is a forlorn-looking illustration of Sigmund Freud doing on the cover of the April 9 *Forbes* magazine? The answer is in Robert Langreth's six-page article, "Patient, Fix Thyself," an explanation of the benefits of cognitive behavioral therapy (CBT).

While not new, Langreth says, this form of talk therapy, whose roots he traces to Albert Ellis, 93, and Aaron Beck, 85, is gaining more believers among patients, therapists and managed care plans. Langreth calls it a "startling revolution in psychological counseling."

It doesn't rely on drugs, is of shorter duration than other forms of psychotherapy and does not dwell on the patient's past. Langreth describes "the essence of CBT: Depression, anxiety and other ills aren't the cause of a cascade of debilitating thoughts and self-loathing—they are, instead, a result of the same. Eliminate bad thoughts and you can short-circuit bad feelings. CBT drops the endless search for past hurts, teaches patients how to prevent negative thoughts from creeping into their minds and coaches them on how to cope."

—*Bruce Rosenstein and Priyanka Dayal*

- Personalization (arbitrary self-blame)—"My boss didn't smile at me in the hallway. I must have screwed up!" In cognitive behavioral therapy, patients learn how to speak to themselves in healthier ways. It's similar to learning a new language—the language of successfully coping with and managing fear. For example, in CBT, people with panic disorder learn to interpret physical symptoms differently. They replace the statement, "My pulse is racing. I'm going to have a panic attack," with "My pulse is beating fast because I just walked up a flight of stairs," or even, "My pulse is beating fast. It will likely slow down in a moment. It has in the past."

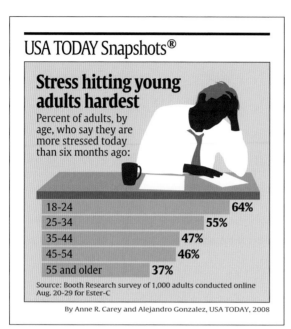

## USA TODAY Snapshots®

### Stress hitting young adults hardest

Percent of adults, by age, who say they are more stressed today than six months ago:

| | |
|---|---|
| 18-24 | **64%** |
| 25-34 | **55%** |
| 35-44 | **47%** |
| 45-54 | **46%** |
| 55 and older | **37%** |

Source: Booth Research survey of 1,000 adults conducted online Aug. 20-29 for Ester-C

By Anne R. Carey and Alejandro Gonzalez, USA TODAY, 2008

By using a new language, a person challenges his or her faulty beliefs about panic attacks, most importantly, the false belief that people can die from panic attacks. Challenging faulty beliefs can help a person with post-traumatic stress disorder identify self-blaming and shame-based beliefs that cause emotional pain and withdrawal from normal life activities. Challenging obsessive thoughts and faulty beliefs can help people with obsessive-compulsive disorder resist their compulsive behaviors. Cognitive strategies aren't enough, however. For people with panic disorder, agoraphobia, obsessive-compulsive disorder, specific phobias, and social phobia, the behavioral piece of cognitive behavioral therapy is especially important.

## BEHAVIORAL STRATEGIES

Habits such as avoiding feared things, people, situations, or even one's own thoughts actually sustain and reinforce anxiety. Exposure-based techniques are the most effective behavioral strategies for helping people overcome avoidance. These techniques work by gradually helping people to confront their fears by placing themselves in the situations they fear. Another important method is exposure and response prevention (ERP), which helps people learn new, more effective responses to anxiety-triggering situations. This method is also called ritual prevention. Just what happens in exposure and response prevention? Exposure is the process of placing yourself in the very situation that triggers fear and dread with the purpose of overcoming the distress the situation causes. Exposure reduces the anxiety and distress of fear-provoking situations through a natural process called habituation.

Here's how it works. Our nervous system naturally goes through the habituation process whenever we get used to something that at first jolts us or causes fear. A good example is seeing a really scary horror movie. The first time you see it, you are surprised, shocked, oe even grossed out. You decide to see it again, and this time, the movie doesn't seem so scary. The shocking parts seem predictable, and the gross parts are not so gross anymore. You decide to sit through the movie a third time, and it's totally boring. The repeated viewing of the same movie has caused your nervous system to say, "Ho hum, I've seen this before." This is like the process of nervous system habituation.

Another example is easing yourself into a swimming pool filled with cold water. Imagine sitting on the edge of a pool and dipping your foot into the cold water. At first, it feels uncomfortably frigid. You want to immediately pull your foot out. But if you keep your foot in the water, after about thirty seconds, something changes. The water feels comfortable on your foot. What changed? Did the water temperature change? No. After prolonged exposure to the cold water, the temperature sensors in your skin got used to, or habituated to, the sensations of the cold water.

The technique of exposure uses this natural process of habituation to help people overcome phobias of all types. Imagine, for example, that you had never learned to swim. As a result, you are fearful of the water, even terrified of it. The very thought of getting within even a

few feet of a swimming pool would be terrifying. Through the process of exposure, your fear could be overcome. First, you walk within a few feet of the swimming pool. You feel immediate discomfort. Your heart races, stomach churns, palms become sweaty, and mouth becomes dry. After a few minutes, the initial fear you felt starts to lessen as your nervous system habituates to the idea of being within a few feet of the dreaded swimming pool.

You now feel braver, so you inch closer to the pool's edge. Again, your fear rises and your heart races, your breathing pace increases, your hands get clammy, and you feel those butterflies in your stomach. You don't move. You stay where you are. After a while, your fear again lessens as you habituate to the idea of being near the pool.

Determined to get into the pool, you then place one toe into the water, and once again the fear rises. But as before, after a few minutes, your nervous system habituates to the water. You submerge your ankle, then your calf, and then your knee. Slowly but gradually, you are in the water up to your waist, thanks to the capacity of your nervous system to adapt to the feared situation through habituation. You have mastered your fear through the use of your brain's natural alarm shut-off mechanism.

Behavioral strategies such as habituation involve small, purposeful steps that lead a person closer to overcoming fear. For someone who fears swimming or large bodies of water, sitting on a dock would be a small step forward in the habituation process.

In a similar way, exposure works to help people with anxiety disorders overcome fears. A therapist will ask a person with an anxiety disorder to place him- or herself in direct contact with the things they fear. The approach is gradual, like moving slowly into the feared swimming pool. The ultimate goal is complete habituation to the feared object or situation. It's important to make certain that the exposure brings up the actual anxious feelings it's designed to help control. The idea is to experience the anxiety and realize that it can be tolerated and lessened without having to do the usual rituals or take other protective measures. For people with phobias, exposure means exposing oneself to feared items. For social phobia, it means exposure to feared social situations. People with panic disorder must gradually expose themselves to situations that trigger panic attacks.

Exposure to the physical sensations associated with the panic attacks may also be necessary. The therapist might assist the person in bringing on the rapid heart rate and heavy breathing, for example, and then help the person tolerate the feelings. With the help of an experienced therapist, imaginal exposure can help a person with post-traumatic stress disorder. Exposure to memories of the traumatic event is combined with cognitive strategies. The therapist helps the person move from "Memories are dangerous" to "I can recall without fear." "The world is a dangerous place" to "I can cope." "I am powerless" to "I have control." "I am incompetent" to "I can make good choices."

For people with PTSD, exposure to real-life situations that bring on anxiety can also be helpful. For example, a person might be avoiding certain areas, such as movie theaters, that bring on irrational fears. By going to movie theaters, the person with PTSD can begin to lose fear of such places. For people with obsessive-compulsive disorder, exposure is only half the story in ERP. The other important component, response prevention, means to actively and purposefully *not* do whatever the person usually feels compelled to do to relieve the immediate anxiety and discomfort of the obsessive thoughts. This may mean not washing hands, not checking the door locks over and over, not counting, or not rethinking a thought "correctly." The idea is to allow the nervous system's natural habituation process to lessen the anxiety of the thought, rather than trying to get anxiety relief through the compulsive behavior.

During exposure therapy, it's important to experience at least a moderate amount of anxiety and continue the exposure long enough for the anxiety to rise and then fall to manageable levels. When habituation occurs, nervous system boredom sets in. The mind has the chance to realize that the feared consequences, such as getting sick or burning the house down, aren't going to happen after all. When exposure is combined with response prevention, more appropriate reactions to the anxiety-provoking thoughts can be learned. Real progress can be made toward overcoming OCD.

## ALONE OR WITH HELP?

Doing ERP is highly challenging. Many people with mild to moderately severe symptoms can do ERP on their own with good results. However, to address more severe OCD symptoms, it's probably a good idea to do ERP with either a trusted friend or best with a licensed therapist trained in this type of treatment. Initially, you can expect to feel very anxious as you confront anxiety-producing situations and block your learned habit of doing rituals in response to the anxiety.

At first, it may be too difficult to resist the ritual. The person with OCD might choose instead to delay the ritual or alter it in small ways, working gradually toward completely stopping. Sometimes it's almost impossible to do real-life exposure and response prevention because the fears involve events that could be impossible to re-create in the present. They might involve things that could possibly happen far off in the future—such as getting sick or causing a car accident. In these cases, imaginal exposure is useful. This means describing your most fear-provoking thought or idea in vivid detail and writing it down on paper as a moment-to-moment narrative. Then you record this three- to five-minute narrative on your cell phone or MP3 player, play it back, and listen to it over and over until habituation occurs.

Treatment with ERP is hard work and requires patience and persistence to be successful. Even after the therapy ends, most people with OCD will need to continue using ERP principles, sometimes for the rest of their lives. Some may even need to return to therapy for booster sessions to increase their ERP skills. While ERP principles are described in several self-help books, it's best to get started with a qualified mental health professional who is specifically trained in the use of ERP for people with OCD. This is especially important for children and teens.

Through imaginal exposure, a person writes down a worst-case scenario, records it, and listens to it until habituation occurs.

# CHAPTER FOUR

# STRESS MANAGEMENT

## ELIZABETH'S STORY

Even as a small child, Elizabeth had been worried and restless. She became panicked whenever her parents were out of her sight—even for a short time. She'd resist her parents' leaving her with a babysitter. For years, bedtime was a disaster. Elizabeth resisted sleeping alone in her own bed well into puberty. As a teen, Elizabeth's worries grew and spread to many different situations. She always focused on what could possibly go wrong in any given situation. For that reason, parties and events at school became reasons for major upheavals at home. She worried about the weather destroying her hair, makeup, and shoes.

When she was involved in helping plan for an event, the stress was almost impossible for her and the entire family. What if she forgot to do something? What if others didn't do their part? Urgent phone calls and e-mails flew between her and her friends. They told her not to worry that everything was okay and taken care of. But still she fretted, called, and e-mailed. When the day of the event came, she couldn't enjoy it because she'd have a stomachache or headache. She'd go anyway and get through the event in a daze, never satisfied with the way things turned out.

Afterward, she'd go home and sleep most of the weekend, exhausted. Then she'd worry that someone was angry with her or hurt by something she'd said at the party or the event. She would tell herself that never again would she be involved in such a thing. But she would get involved again.

Elizabeth's restlessness and irritability leading up to events kept the entire family on edge. They felt as if they had to be constantly on alert, careful not to say something that would agitate or irritate her. After the event, their job was to cheer her up and reassure her that everything was fine. Elizabeth also worried about family problems. When she overheard an argument between her parents, she became convinced that they were getting a divorce. She called her mother's sister and begged her to intervene. It took a great deal of heated discussion to convince her that her parents had a healthy marriage. Their arguments were normal, and her parents had no plans for divorce. Even after things had calmed down for the rest of the family, Elizabeth spent a great deal of time worrying about her parents' marriage. What would happen to her and her brothers if they were to divorce? With whom would she live?

She had difficulty concentrating on her schoolwork, and her grades fell. When she came home with her first C on a history test, she worried that she would fail the class. What if this was only the first bad grade of many and she failed all her classes? What if she didn't graduate from high school? Her worries always went to the extreme.

The more she worried, the worse Elizabeth's stomachaches and headaches became. Her mother made an appointment with the family doctor. Elizabeth worried that she had a horrible disease. If the stomachaches and headaches were of concern enough to see the doctor, then maybe she had something seriously wrong with her. The doctor ran tests and told her and her mother the headaches were migraines. He prescribed migraine medication for Elizabeth. But he was even more concerned about the restlessness, fatigue, worrying, and anxiety. He referred her to a psychiatrist, who diagnosed her with general anxiety disorder.

## STRESS AND YOU

In addition to cognitive behavioral therapy and medications, therapists often recommend lifestyle changes to relieve anxiety and distress. These lifestyle changes can help us all manage the stress of daily living. Whether or not you have an anxiety disorder, you can benefit from the following stress management tools. Graduating

from high school, changing your sleeping pattern, moving to a new town, getting arrested, going on vacation, and changing schools—these are all possible sources, or triggers, of stress.

Did you notice that they all involve change? Almost any change, positive or negative, causes stress. All stress is not necessarily bad. Stress prompts our brain's fight-or-flight response, part of a range of biological responses that are essential to successfully facing life's challenges, including change. Some responses are turned on for long periods, especially in response to situations involving major changes that feel unpredictable and uncontrollable—like illness in the family, sudden trauma, or financial hardship. These responses take a toll on the body. Excessive stress can contribute to heart disease, high blood pressure, diabetes, headaches, ulcers, chronic diarrhea, muscle tension, and many other physical ailments. Living with situations that severely challenge our capacity to cope, that feel uncontrollable or unpredictable, can potentially result in a chronic psychological and/or physical problem. We can settle into an almost constant state of moderate or low-level stress.

Spending time with friends can be a great way to relieve stress.

Since stress can have a negative impact on our bodies, it's important to give ourselves breaks from stress. The goal isn't to eliminate all stress, however. That would make life boring. We need to add positive stress, or what is called eustress, to our lives. Examples of eustress are exercise, cheering a favorite team, getting together with friends, and other enjoyable activities. The goals are to eliminate distress, add eustress, and give ourselves breaks from stress.

# How the body responds

Stress can manifest itself in a number of physical illnesses as well as emotional problems. Various parts of the body can be affected. More information is available from the American Institute of Stress, www.stress.org.

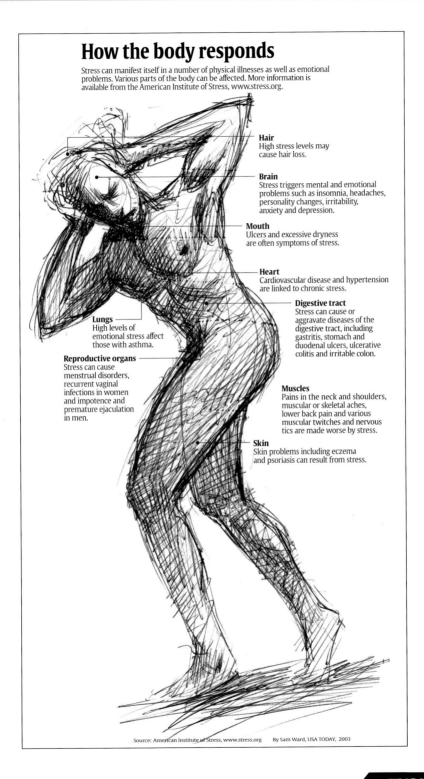

**Hair**
High stress levels may cause hair loss.

**Brain**
Stress triggers mental and emotional problems such as insomnia, headaches, personality changes, irritability, anxiety and depression.

**Mouth**
Ulcers and excessive dryness are often symptoms of stress.

**Heart**
Cardiovascular disease and hypertension are linked to chronic stress.

**Digestive tract**
Stress can cause or aggravate diseases of the digestive tract, including gastritis, stomach and duodenal ulcers, ulcerative colitis and irritable colon.

**Lungs**
High levels of emotional stress affect those with asthma.

**Reproductive organs**
Stress can cause menstrual disorders, recurrent vaginal infections in women and impotence and premature ejaculation in men.

**Muscles**
Pains in the neck and shoulders, muscular or skeletal aches, lower back pain and various muscular twitches and nervous tics are made worse by stress.

**Skin**
Skin problems including eczema and psoriasis can result from stress.

Source: American Institute of Stress, www.stress.org    By Sam Ward, USA TODAY, 2003

May 27, 2003

From the Pages of USA TODAY

# Is all that stress killing you?; Probably. But taking stock can mitigate the damage.

Adults can pay a high price for chronic distress. Long-term stress releases brain chemicals that can be toxic, contributing to ailments as minor as headaches and as critical as heart attacks, says Paul Rosch, clinical professor of medicine and psychiatry at New York Medical College and president of the American Institute of Stress.

About 60% of visits to health care professionals are "in the stress-related, mind-body realm," worsening problems such as sexual performance and insomnia, says Herbert Benson, president of the Mind/Body Medical Institute and co-author of *The Breakout Principle*. More information is at www.mbmi.org.

"Stress is different for each one of us," Rosch says. Giving a speech can be terrifying for some but a delight for those who love being the center of attention.

Just as there is no definition of stress common to all, there is no one correct way to cope with it. "No strategy for dealing with stress is a panacea [cure]. You have to find out what works for you," Rosch says.

Researchers don't talk about eliminating stress. "Stress is an unavoidable consequence of life, of the human condition," Rosch says. And some of it is good,

sparking necessary action such as reacting to danger or improving—to a point—performance and productivity.

But chronic stress can leach the joy from daily living. Researchers are finding new clues to how to handle it, and prevention is proving to be significant.

The core cause of much stress is the sense one is not in the driver's seat. "All the clinical and lab research shows that the perception of not having control is very stressful," Rosch says. "The way to turn a stressful incident into something that is not stressful is to regain a sense of control over it."

Though you may not control events, experts say you can control your reactions.

To restore a sense of control, Rosch suggests, "make a list of all the things that tick you off" and that create daily stress. Then decide which ones you can do something about. "What could you do with that commute that takes an hour a day? You could go to the boss and tell him you have to change your hours. Or that you can do some of your work from home."

If that doesn't work, think of new ways to use the commute time, perhaps listening to books on tape in the car, he says. This type of thinking is called "reframing."

Also list the things you cannot change, Rosch says, and have somebody check both lists. You may get suggestions for moving some minuses to the plus column. When you get down to bedrock, to those few stressors that can't be changed, accept them and move on, Rosch says.

Benson and others also say negative patterns of thought may become the cause of chronic stress. Often they can be traced to "nagging anxieties, stress-related emotional baggage or circular, obsessive mental tapes" that are recorded in the mind in early childhood, Benson says.

The goal of stress experts is to break that cycle. In *The Breakout Principle*, Benson combines science and self-help. He suggests "turning on a natural inner switch to sever [cut off] those past mental patterns." With practice, that signal, or "trigger," which can be as simple as taking a brisk walk, actually turns on different, calming brain chemicals.

[Denver psychiatrist Paul] Dobransky talks about filtering out the bad messages. He refers to setting "personal boundaries" that "are our ultimate protection against stress." Like countries, the boundaries have "customs and immigration services whose purpose is to keep out what is bad for us and let in what is good."

It takes discipline, commitment and practice to build such boundaries, Dobransky says. And that is difficult to accomplish in an era that worships "the quick fix."

Some of the anxious do need professional help to set stress down. But the trend among many researchers is to emphasize the natural strengths of individuals. They can learn, Rosch says, that "maybe I can't fight. Maybe I can't take flight. But I can learn to go with the flow."

—*Karen S. Peterson*

## Ways to calm the mind

Stress experts offer a range of activities and relaxation techniques to help unwind. They include:

- Visualization. "Imagining yourself taking a hot bath, strolling a beach, or sitting in a quiet meadow can markedly shift both your mind state and physiology toward stillness."
- Progressive muscle relaxation. This technique achieves "deep relaxation by gradually tensing and then releasing muscle groups throughout the body: eyes, jaw, neck, shoulders, arms, back, chest, abdomen, pelvis, buttocks, legs and feet." Take a slow, deep breath when allowing the muscles to relax.
- Spiritual growth and prayer. Consider whether spiritual activities might help. They could include religious services, joining a spiritual community, regular prayer or a deeper commitment to a spiritual life.
- Worry time. Set aside 15 to 30 minutes to actively worry about problems from the past 24 hours. "At any other time during the day when you start to worry, say to yourself, 'STOP. Save it for worry time.'"

# TAKE CONTROL OF YOUR THOUGHTS

Take a moment to think about what you consider stressful. Events and situations, such as failing an important test, moving to a new school, or breaking up with a girlfriend or boyfriend may trigger extreme feelings of stress or anxiety. Someone else may consider such events as only a challenge. Still others might view such events as just a part of everyday life. Stress comes when you perceive something as a threat to your physical or psychological well-being and you believe that you can't cope with the threat. The key word here is *perceive*. Events do not cause stress. Instead, it is our perception of those events, our learned beliefs about them, that result in stress and anxiety. Once you recognize this, you are in a position to choose how you look at life and take steps toward reducing stress. When you notice signs of stress in your body—nervousness, anger, worry, headaches, back pain, indigestion, etc.—stop and take a deep breath or two. Observe your negative thoughts. Is there a more positive way of looking at the stress-causing situation? Can you see it as a challenge or an opportunity for growth? Can you see the humor in the situation? It's hard to be stressed when you're smiling or laughing.

If the worry is caused by something serious—such as illness or death—look for ways to share and manage your burden by involving others. Talk to a trusted friend, family member, or other adult. Ask for help. If you don't have the support of family and friends, look for a trusted adult at school or at your church or in one of your after-school activities. No matter what, begin to build and grow a network of support now so it is there when you need it in the future.

If worry is a problem, saying to yourself, "Stop worrying!" just doesn't work. Instead, try scheduling ten to thirty minutes every day for worrying. The best time is toward the end of the day, when you've likely collected some things to worry about. Don't make it so late in the day that you're feeling tired. Fatigue can increase worry and anxiety.

Make certain your worry time is not at bedtime so it doesn't disturb your sleep. The trick is to limit yourself to worrying only during that time. When worries pop up before your worry time, write them down on a "Worry List" to get them out of your mind until later in the day. This way, instead of saying "Stop!" you're saying "Wait." During your worry time, do nothing but worry. When your mind wanders, bring it back to worrying. The important thing is to postpone worry the rest of the day. With time, you'll probably become bored with your worries and eventually want to lessen your worry time.

In addition, you can cut down on your worries by getting more organized. Having clear goals with plans to achieve those goals will give you much less to worry about. Prepare ahead for the next day and the next week, make lists, and keep an organizer. Ask friends for tips on how they stay organized. Do whatever it takes to keep organized.

Test your worries. While many things are out of our control, we often worry about things we can actually do something about. Ask yourself if you can do anything about a specific worry on your list. Write down all the options that come to mind and then choose a plan of action. Write down the steps you'll take to solve the problem and then carry out the plan. If it doesn't work, choose another plan. It might help to consult with trusted friends, family members, or advisers. And remember to be careful about not talking your plans and worries to death. There's a point when talking about a problem stops being helpful and begins to increase stress. At this point, stop discussing it unless you come up with a new aspect or possible solution. When you stop talking about a problem, you tend to dwell on it less.

## RELAXATION

Taking time out for relaxing activities, such as listening to music, reading books for pleasure, talking with friends, and reflecting on spiritual matters, gives our minds and bodies breaks from negative stress. Recreational activities, community involvement, and exercise can also give us opportunities to take a break from stress. If we fill our lives with too many activities, however, they begin to add stress. Balance is key to effective stress management. The above activities are relaxing.

Another technique, called the relaxation response, is a form of relaxation that has a more profound physical effect on the body. Relaxation response—the opposite of stress response—was first described by Herbert Benson in the 1970s. It refers to a state of deep relaxation when heart rate, respiration, blood pressure, and muscle tension are all decreased. Using relaxation techniques to induce a state of deep relaxation is an option for people who need to give their bodies a break from excess negative stress. It can reduce anxiety and fatigue, increase energy, and improve productivity, memory, and concentration.

Getting involved in a community event such as a biking fund-raiser helps people relax by encouraging them to focus on helping others.

Spending twenty to thirty minutes a day in a state of relaxation helps reduce stress during the rest of the day. With practice, a person can also relax more easily throughout the day, producing even more stress reduction. Various relaxation techniques are described in numerous books. The most common techniques include progressive muscle relaxation, abdominal breathing, visualization, meditation, guided imagery, and biofeedback. An easy and effective relaxation exercise is simply to observe and change your breathing pattern. When people are anxious, they tend to breathe more shallowly and rapidly from the chest. Relaxed breathing, however, is slower and deeper and is centered in the abdomen.

Take a few moments to observe your breathing right now. Sit or lie down with your hand placed on your abdomen, just below your ribs. Does your abdomen or your chest move up when you inhale (breathe in)? Relax your abdominal muscles and breathe in slowly and deeply through your nose so that your abdomen rises. Pause, and then exhale (breathe out) slowly and completely through your nose. Your hand on your abdomen should go up as you inhale and down as you exhale. Breathe in, pause, and breathe out. Do this gently, slowly, and smoothly about ten times. After practicing abdominal breathing daily at home, you'll be able to instantly change to a more relaxed breathing pattern when you find yourself breathing anxiously from your chest.

## TAKE CARE OF YOUR BODY

The human mind and body are very closely connected. You can use this fact to help manage anxiety. For example, a healthy diet can reduce your anxiety and stress. But be prepared: short-term sacrifices may appear to be anxiety-provoking. If you're unwilling or unable to make all the changes, start with a few and build on your success. A stress-reducing diet is well balanced and high in fruits and vegetables. It's low in refined carbohydrates—foods such as potato chips, white bread, cakes, pies, and candy. Instead, eat complex carbohydrates, such as whole grain bread and cereals, brown rice, and vegetables. A stress-reducing diet is also low in saturated fats such as butter and lard. Healthier sources of fat are nuts and monounsaturated oils—olive and canola oils, for example. Healthy sources of protein include fish, beans, soy products, and legumes. This type of diet is good for your heart and brain, guards against cancer and premature aging, and can help you maintain a healthy weight or even lose weight.

## AVOID STIMULANTS

Some foods and beverages can make anxiety worse. Caffeine has a stimulating effect, for example, and produces the same effects as stress on your body. Cutting back or eliminating caffeine from your diet can reduce restlessness, irritability, and difficulty sleeping. Caffeine can be found in coffee, tea, soda, chocolate, and some over-the-counter medications. Abrupt withdrawal from caffeine may cause headache, fatigue, and depression. Most people find it easier to taper off caffeine gradually.

Nicotine is also a stimulant. You may think smoking is relaxing, but the physical response of stimulation from

Coffee and other caffeinated beverages can make a person more anxious. Because it is a stimulant, caffeine can have the same effects on the body as stress.

nicotine is the opposite of relaxation. While quitting smoking can be stressful, the long-term result is stress reduction and a healthier body. Some nonprescription and prescription medications contain stimulants and may also increase anxiety. Pseudoephedrine, often found in cold and allergy preparations, can leave you feeling restless and nervous. Alcoholic beverages and all illegal drugs should be avoided. Illegal stimulants such as ephedra, amphetamines, and cocaine are especially dangerous for people at risk for panic attacks and anxiety disorders.

## EXERCISE

Physical exercise is an example of the eustress that we need in our lives. Exercise improves your sense of well-being by stimulating the production of endorphins, natural pain-reducing and mood-moderating chemicals. Exercise enhances oxygenation of the blood and brain. With more oxygen in the blood and brain, we are better able to concentrate, remember things, and remain alert. Exercise also reduces muscle tension, improves blood circulation and digestion, and reduces blood pressure.

Exercise can be especially helpful for people with depression and anxiety disorders. People with panic disorder sometimes avoid exercise that raises their heart rate. They fear that the rapid heart rate might trigger a panic attack. Gradually increasing the amount of or the intensity of exercise along with challenging your faulty beliefs about the likelihood of having a panic attack when normal heartbeat acceleration occurs can help people with panic disorder benefit from exercise. They will gradually feel less fearful of the physical aspects of panic attacks. Aerobic exercise is a good option for reducing stress, anxiety, and muscle tension. It also improves cardiovascular fitness. Aerobic exercise is any physical activity that raises your heart rate and increases the efficiency of oxygen intake by the body. This type of exercise includes running, brisk walking, swimming, outdoor cycling, stationary biking, or vigorous dancing. Anaerobic exercise involves short bursts of activity and builds muscle. This form of exercise includes weight lifting and short-distance swimming or sprinting. The important thing is to develop an exercise program that you enjoy. Consistency is the most important factor. Aim for twenty to thirty minutes four to five times a week—and don't fret if you miss a day or two.

## REST AND LAUGHTER

In addition to nourishment and exercise, your body needs rest. Sleep provides rest and rejuvenation for your brain, your mind, and your body. Inadequate sleep has a negative effect on the neurotransmitters GABA and serotonin. This causes anxiety and stress, which makes it even more difficult to sleep. The best way to avoid this cycle is to do everything possible to maintain good sleep habits. The amount of sleep you need is an individual matter. If you are tired or sleepy during the day, have an overwhelming desire to take a nap, or are not as alert as you think you should be, you probably need more sleep. A few tips will improve your sleeping habits and help reduce your stress. Try to get up at the same time and go to bed at the same time every day. Pay attention to your body's cues at night and go to bed when you first feel tired. If you wait much longer, you will create stress and overstimulation, which can make it harder to fall asleep.

Develop a relaxing bedtime routine by reducing noise, light, stimulation, and activity before you go to bed. Avoid caffeine in the evening, as well as alcohol. Alcohol may seem relaxing, but it actually disrupts the sleep pattern. So does watching television and looking at computer screens and texting. If possible, get computers and cell phones out of your room at night. A light snack before bed can be helpful. Regular exercise improves sleep, but be sure to complete your exercise routine a few hours before bedtime. If you go to bed and can't sleep, don't just lie there. Get up and do something relaxing—such as reading or listening to quiet music—in another room. Keep in mind that texting and computer work aren't relaxing activities.

Our minds and bodies need more rest than what we get from sleep. So spend some time daily on relaxing activities. Take an extended break every week for rest and recreation and periodically take a vacation. What's a vacation? Be creative! A vacation can be two weeks visiting family, a week at a theme park or camp, or several days between work and the start of a new school year relaxing and hanging out with friends. Don't stop there though. When you recognize signs of stress in your body, give yourself extra breaks. Take a short walk or stand up and stretch your legs or spend five minutes playing a computer game.

Perhaps the ultimate rest for the body and mind is humor. Laughter decreases stress and increases our tolerance for pain. It can temporarily lift anxiety and depression, relieve stress, and help us connect with others. More importantly, humor and laughter help us perceive life differently. Seeing the humor in situations makes the situations less threatening and lowers our stress.

## SET GOALS

Stress sometimes comes from feeling a lack of fulfillment. We all need to find a sense of purpose and to be working toward achieving life goals. This search for purpose is a lifetime journey. When we stop our search and just stumble through life, we become more vulnerable to anxiety and stress. Having well-defined goals and plans reduces stress. Take a moment and list your short-term goals, things you'd like to achieve today or in the next few weeks or months. Then list your long-term goals, things you'd like to achieve during your lifetime. Now list ideas from this chapter that can help you reduce negative stress. You'll find that many of them will also help you achieve many of your goals. The main point is that working toward your goals will lower stress, and the things that can further lower stress will help you achieve your goals.

## ANXIETY AND STRESS RELIEF: WHAT *DOESN'T* WORK

For many reasons, people often try other methods to relieve anxiety and stress first. Some of these methods seem harmless. However, they may keep a person from trying more effective measures. Other attempts to relieve anxiety and stress can be quite dangerous, even life-threatening. Below is a list of some of the ineffective ways people try to cope with anxiety and stress. You've probably tried at least one of these measures yourself, and you've probably seen others using every one of them to try to handle the stress in their lives.

### STRESS EATING

Eating unhealthy foods, eating too much, or eating too little—you get the idea. Some people overeat when they're under stress, while others practically stop eating. Many treat themselves to comfort foods such as chips and ice cream and other desserts when they're upset or under stress. From what you've learned in the last chapter, you know that this only increases anxiety and stress. Coffee, tea, and many sodas contain a very powerful nervous system stimulant—caffeine—which can aggravate anxiety and stress if consumed in excessive quantities. The solution is to be moderate in your eating habits and to plan ahead. Substitute healthier foods for comfort foods and eat smaller servings. Even better, don't use food for comfort. Be prepared with truly effective measures to help you through the rough spots in life. Enjoy coffee drinks with your friends, but make it a decaf latte with skim milk or soy milk. Explore the world of herbal teas.

## EXCESSIVE SHOPPING, INTERNET SURFING, GAMBLING, AND OTHER BEHAVIORS

Shopping, playing video games, surfing the Internet, texting, watching TV, and many other activities can be relaxing in reasonable doses. You can zone out and lose yourself in the activity. Other activities, including gambling, can also be a relaxing form of entertainment for some people. However, problem and pathological (unhealthy, addictive) gambling can severely strain finances and relationships and add to a person's stress and anxiety.

Anything done to excess can lead people to overlook important chores, perform poorly at school and at work, spend too much money, or ignore important relationships. When this happens, the activity becomes stressful—

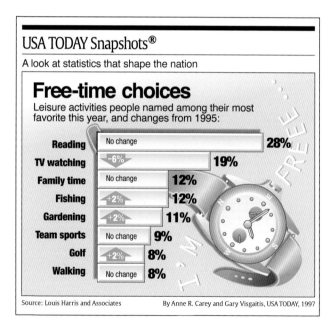

USA TODAY Snapshots®

A look at statistics that shape the nation

**Free-time choices**

Leisure activities people named among their most favorite this year, and changes from 1995:

| Activity | Change | Percent |
|---|---|---|
| Reading | No change | 28% |
| TV watching | -6% | 19% |
| Family time | No change | 12% |
| Fishing | +2% | 12% |
| Gardening | +2% | 11% |
| Team sports | No change | 9% |
| Golf | +2% | 8% |
| Walking | No change | 8% |

Source: Louis Harris and Associates    By Anne R. Carey and Gary Visgaitis, USA TODAY, 1997

even addictive—rather than relaxing. When you are using positive stress management skills, you won't be as likely to rely on excessive or addictive activities to relieve stress and anxiety.

October 5, 2009

From the Pages of USA TODAY

# Pull yourself away from that iPhone and read this story

## Can't? Then you may be addicted to Apple's ubiquitous apps

Most people start their day with a cup of coffee, a shower, a good stretch. Beth Akins rolls over, grabs her iPhone and fires up Shake & Spell, her favorite iPhone app game.

"I usually play before I even get out of bed," says Akins, 54, of Louisville [Kentucky], who says a day without Shake & Spell leaves her with feelings of withdrawal. "I play every day."

Apps is short for computer maker Apple's applications, and it refers to the scores of games and services that iPhone or iPod touch owners can download and interact with. There are 85,000 different apps for Akins and the other 50 million users around the world.

### Apps and your health

People may wonder what the iPhone apps obsession is driven by as they witness "i" users strolling down work hallways and streets "apping" and bumping into others. And what about all those children seen manically poking away at their parents' iPhone games in doctors' offices and cashier lines across the country? What is app addiction doing to people's health?

"Clearly, the reward circuitry in the brain is getting something out of it," says Marina Picciotto, professor of psychiatry, neurobiology and pharmacology at Yale University [in Connecticut].

She says there is no research on the impact of apps on health yet.

"Obviously, what it's doing to our health, it's too early to tell. There are a few parallels we can make from other addictions, like compulsive shopping. The consequences can be bad—credit debt, time lost."

One attraction: Apps are cheap (sometimes free), and the payback is fast.

There are apps that can help you avoid traffic jams, one that walks you through the steps of making a perfect latte, and another that tracks flu outbreaks. There are sports apps galore and scores of games.

Anish Acharya, 30, co-founder of SocialDeck, the company that invented Akin's beloved Shake & Spell, a Boggle-like game in which the goal is to shake up 16 little squares with letters and then spell as many words as possible in three minutes, says the draw can be a combination of social and competitive rewards.

"For some people it's just about winning and getting to the top of the leader board. For others it's an interaction with a stranger," he says. "And for others, it's just about killing 10 minutes in the line at the butcher's shop."

For Akins, her app obsession keeps her connected with her sister, who is homebound in Athens, Ga., waiting for a lung transplant. "She can't travel, so I bought her an iPhone so she could play with me," Akins says.

## Are they taking over?

Though some research suggests playing brain games can boost cognitive [thinking] power, the downside of app overuse can include the time it takes away from family, friends, tasks such as getting your children to school on time, and health needs such as sleeping, Picciotto says.

Users should keep tabs on whether apps are taking over their real lives, says Hilarie Cash, a psychotherapist and co-founder of reStart, a Fall City, Wash.-based Internet-addiction recovery center that opened this summer and is the first of its kind.

"If you are spending two hours or more a day engaged with your digital equipment and it's not for work- or homework-related reasons, then you've got cause for alarm," Cash says.

Jim Sun, 47, a father of four from Anaheim, Calif., has downloaded about 60 apps to his iPod touch. They've replaced TV and some family time, Sun says, "and definitely sleep."

Over-apping may overwhelm the brain, says Gary Small, author of iBrain and professor of psychiatry and biobehavioral sciences at the University of California's (Los Angeles) David Geffen School of Medicine.

"When we're constantly scanning the environment, waiting for the next bit of info from our devices, I think it puts our brain into a stressful state, and stress is not good for the brain," Small says.

## The body's in play, too

App abuse can have purely physical repercussions, too, such as carpal tunnel from repetitive hand movements, Picciotto says.

Akins says her neck aches after too many games in a row.

Parents rave about how handy an app game is when kids get fidgety, but there's no research yet on whether some of the content might be inappropriate for children, Picciotto says.

Bert Vabre, 45, of Oakland, N.J., has downloaded about 50 apps, from financial services to sports to games for his kids. "My son likes iMafia. He probably shouldn't be playing that one," Vabre says with a chuckle.

And what happens to app addicts when an iPhone accidentally falls into a puddle or is left behind? One online commenter recently posted on MacRumors that he went to lunch without the device and felt naked.

Small says withdrawal feelings suggest dopamine receptors in the brain aren't getting their fix.

Maybe someone will come up with an app for what to do when you forget your iPhone.

—*Mary Brophy Marcus*

## GETTING ANGRY

Sometimes stress results when emotions such as anger, resentment, and jealousy toward others aren't expressed directly or appropriately. Storing these emotions, locking them up inside, can result in increased distress, moodiness, and even depression. On the other hand, giving free rein to these emotions in the form of rants, tantrums, aggressive behavior, bullying, or engaging in high-risk behaviors can be destructive and even dangerous to yourself and those around you. Learn to communicate painful feelings such as anger honestly, directly, and respectfully with others. It can be a great stress reliever. If you find yourself unable to do this on your own, seek the confidential guidance of a mental health counselor who is trained in working with teenagers. A counselor can be an excellent resource for your emotional health. That person can help you to get in touch with and express your feelings appropriately.

## ISOLATION

Taking an occasional break from the stress and pressures of daily life is not just desirable. It's also an important part of maintaining emotional health and well-being. Take time out for fun, reflection, rest, relaxation, vacation, or any enjoyable activity. Some forms of

**USA TODAY Snapshots®**

**How some teens registered despair**
Percentage of high school students who say they felt so hopeless that they made a suicide plan in the past year:

Male
**14.1%**

Female
**18.9%**

Source: 2003 Youth Risk Behavior Survey, Centers for Disease Control and Prevention

By Cristina Abello and Sam Ward, USA TODAY, 2005

diversion—such as isolating yourself from friends, family, and usual activities; sleeping too much; or missing school, work, and other obligations—are not healthy. When this is happening, there could be a problem. Social withdrawal is one of the symptoms of depression, which is common among teens and adults with anxiety disorders.

Clinically significant depression is characterized by symptoms such as persistent and strong feelings of sadness, hopelessness, and helplessness; impaired sleep; lack of energy; crying or frequent tearfulness; loss of interest in normal activities; impaired appetite; weight loss or gain; and suicidal feelings or thoughts. If you or anyone you know has any of these symptoms, tell your parent, a doctor, or a counselor right away. If you or someone you know has suicidal thoughts, even occasionally, seek help now.

Most cities and towns have a suicide hotline that can help you. Call the National Suicide Prevention Lifeline at 1-800-273-TALK (8255), a free, twenty-four-hour hotline available to anyone in suicidal crisis or emotional distress. Your call will be routed to the crisis center nearest to you. Or visit the organization's website at www.suicidepreventionlifeline.org/.

## DRUGGING AND DRINKING

People drink or take drugs for many reasons, including relieving boredom and loneliness and fitting in with others. They may also be trying to cope with negative feelings such as anxiety, fear, depression, grief, frustration, anger, shame, and guilt. At first alcohol or drugs may seem to provide relief from these unpleasant emotions. Occasional, experimental recreational use of drugs and alcohol may appear harmless. Under the right circumstances, however, a persistent pattern of use and eventual misuse—including abuse and even addiction—can develop. A young person who is considering taking illegal drugs or alcohol should think twice.

January 11, 2000

From the Pages of USA TODAY

# Mental misery besieges many

About 20 million Americans suffer from recurrent bouts of major depression, studies show. And although research is promising, experts still aren't sure who is vulnerable or exactly how to treat it."

The need for research in this area is critical," says Martin Keller, a pioneering researcher at Brown University [in Rhode Island].

As mental health professionals pursue answers, the costs of major depression to sufferers and to society remain huge, Keller says. "Estimates are that the economic costs . . . in the United States are more than $53 billion a year."

And the personal risk is high: Major depressive disorders account for about 20% to 35% of suicides, says the recent study *Mental Health: A Report of the Surgeon General.*

Obviously, this is not some version of the post-holiday blues. Recurring depression means repeated plunges into an abyss [dark place], with profound feelings of despair and loss of interest in life, plus debilitating physical effects such as insomnia.

The causes of depression include genetic, biological, personality and environmental factors. One bout is bad enough. But without any treatment, 80% to 90% of those who suffer a single battle with serious depression will have a second attack within two years, the surgeon general's report says. Toughest of all for sufferers: Even with treatment, large numbers will have repeated episodes.

Mental health professionals and researchers emphasize there is hope. "The good news is that we have treatments that are effective in modifying long-term or major depression, prolonging recovery and maintaining wellness," says Charles Reynolds, a researcher and psychiatrist with the University of Pittsburgh School of Medicine [in Pennsylvania].

The big guns in the treatment of recurrent depression are a variety of antidepressant drugs. New ones are continually being researched. But they are not foolproof. Patients treated for a major depressive episode with medications have a 30% chance of having a second one, says Jesse Rosenthal, chief psychopharmacologist at Beth Israel Medical Center in New York.

And it takes a skilled practitioner to monitor drug use, to decide what antidepressant at what dose to be taken for how long and whether a mood stabilizer also is needed."

Drugs will suppress the depression, but the vulnerability is still there under the surface," cautions psychiatrist Frederick Goodwin, former director of the National Institute of Mental Health.

Goodwin suggests medications be taken for a year after symptoms subside to prevent relapse, then withdrawal from the drugs should be slow. Some patients may need medication indefinitely, and it is often better to stay on it than continue to stop and start.

Goodwin, Keller and others say long-term, maintenance drug therapy might be considered with:

- A first depressive episode before age 30 or after 60.
- A family history of serious depression.
- Two episodes separated by no more than two years.
- A third episode.
- Long-lasting episodes.
- Poor control of symptoms during continued therapy.
- The presence of substance abuse or an anxiety disorder. Instead of just relying on drugs, researchers are trying other routes to block recurrence.

Jackie Gollan, working with Neil Jacobson of the University of Washington in Seattle, found that personality factors can make a difference. In her small study of patients followed for two years after a major depressive episode, 44% battled the illness again.

Gollan's patients had been treated with cognitive behavior therapy (CBT). CBT helps patients change negative thought patterns that contribute to depression to more positive ones. Gollan finds patients who are aggressive and those who are loners are at increased risk—traits that make getting emotional support from other people more difficult.

Many practitioners are enthusiastic about psychotherapies such as CBT that help patients learn coping skills for everyday life, part of keeping depression at bay.

The most effective treatment seems to be a combination of drugs with psychotherapy, experts say.

Researcher Ellen Frank of the University of Pittsburgh finds that medication plus psychotherapy leads to an 80% chance of staying well for three years. Her work is supported by a grant from the National Institute of Mental Health.

Fifty percent of a subset of Frank's female patients get well on just psychotherapy. "And if therapy alone doesn't cut it, adding medication to the treatment then seems to work for about 80% of the remaining half," she says.

For now, the key for sufferers and their family members and friends, Keller says, is to "be tuned in to the earliest symptoms of return. The sooner you catch it, the easier it is to treat."

—*Karen S. Peterson*

Many Americans suffer from depression. A range of treatment options can help people manage this condition.

Besides the risk of dependence and addiction, other costs of alcohol and drug use include:

- Being arrested for possession of illegal drugs, driving while under the influence of alcohol or drugs (DUI), and other substance use-related offenses
- Impaired ability to drive or operate machinery
- Temporary physical discomfort after using the substance—headache, stomachache, vomiting, dizziness, etc.
- Possible worsening of an existing anxiety disorder, depression, or physical disorder as a result of use of alcohol or drugs
- Interference with school, work, and social life. When habitual use takes over, expect your grades and social life to go downhill. If you are under the influence of habitual drug and alcohol use, tardiness to school and work is the norm.
- Sleep difficulties caused by certain substances, such as amphetamines.
- When the high is over, added stress. You'll still have the same problems you did before, with the potential for adding yet another problem (drug or alcohol abuse) to your already stressed-out life.

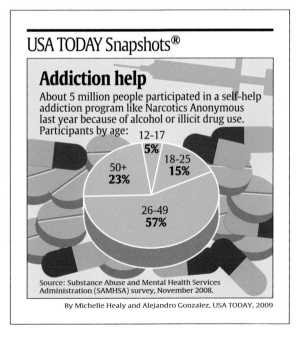

**USA TODAY Snapshots®**

**Addiction help**

About 5 million people participated in a self-help addiction program like Narcotics Anonymous last year because of alcohol or illicit drug use. Participants by age:

- 12-17 **5%**
- 18-25 **15%**
- 50+ **23%**
- 26-49 **57%**

Source: Substance Abuse and Mental Health Services Administration (SAMHSA) survey, November 2008.

By Michelle Healy and Alejandro Gonzalez, USA TODAY, 2009

- Short-term memory loss and overall loss of motivation to succeed and be productive, caused by some drugs such as marijuana
- Alienation from family and friends, caused by a lifestyle of drug and alcohol abuse
- A severe strain on your budget, resulting in financial difficulties

It may be obvious that there are many risks associated with a lifestyle of drug and alcohol use. For teens, alcohol use carries additional costs because its use is illegal. Arrests add unneeded stress and stigma that can last a lifetime. When you consider the legal hassles for teens, it's hard to see any benefits from the use of drugs or alcohol. For those with anxiety disorders, the use of illegal drugs or alcohol has further costs. Drugs and alcohol make the condition worse and typically lead people to postpone seeking and attaining effective medical treatment.

# CHAPTER FIVE

# YOU CAN BEAT AN ANXIETY DISORDER

The young people you've met in this book represent millions of people who are gaining control of their anxiety disorders. They received cognitive behavioral therapy to help them better manage their anxiety and live free of its limitations. Some have also used medication to help reduce their anxiety symptoms. Let's look at some of the things they've learned along the way.

## CAROL: PANIC DISORDER WITH AGORAPHOBIA

*When Carol began to have panic attacks, she put away her dreams of college. She couldn't even go out of the house alone. The attacks would hit her out of the blue, scaring her and everyone around her. The horrible tightness in her chest, shortness of breath, dizziness, and racing heart made her feel sure she was having a heart attack. Even after the doctor, her parents, and the therapist reassured her, it was hard to shake the thought, "I'm dying, I'm having a heart attack. I'll stop breathing any moment."*

*In therapy, Carol learned to interpret her physical symptoms differently. She*

USA TODAY Snapshots®

A look at statistics that shape our lives

**Frowning takes muscle**

The number of muscles it takes to:

34 — Frown

17 — Smile

Source: Impulse Research for Oscar Mayer    By Cindy Hall and Genevieve Lynn, USA TODAY, 1999

challenged her internal thoughts, questioning them. "Could there be another reason for my heart beating fast? Perhaps I was walking fast." Then she waited to see if the symptoms went away. Sure enough, they always did go away. She didn't have a heart attack or die. She also began a moderate exercise routine, first walking and then swimming. As she increased her exercise, she became less fearful of having a fast pulse. Carol graduated with her class and then took one class at the community college the following fall before enrolling full-time.

## MAGGIE: SOCIAL PHOBIA

Maggie felt most comfortable at home. Even there, she felt anxious and nervous just thinking about having to go to school. She was afraid of being called on in class and avoided talking to the other students. Maggie wanted to make friends but didn't know what to talk about and felt sure she'd embarrass herself. Worried because she was becoming quieter and even seemed depressed, her mother took her to a therapist, who challenged her to do the things she feared the most: speak up in class and even start conversations with boys. It was difficult at first, much too difficult, but after she had been on medication for five weeks, she became more willing to take chances. Maggie knew she would never become a social butterfly, but she made some friends, went out on a few dates, and interviewed for a summer job.

## JOSÉ: SOCIAL PHOBIA

Despite all his accomplishments, José felt as if he was hiding a secret. He had a deep fear of speaking. How could a person who was a star on the debate team, who hoped to build a career around speaking, have a fear of speaking? he wondered. José continued to participate on the debate team, but his performance suffered. With each debate, he was afraid that

Life
SECTION D
LIFE.USATODAY.COM

**April 26, 2010**

From the Pages of USA TODAY

# Exercise vs. anxiety
## *It's rarely prescribed but a good option, experts say*

Most people seeking treatment for depression or anxiety face two choices: medication or psychotherapy. But there's a third choice that is rarely prescribed, though it comes with few side effects, low costs and a list of added benefits, advocates say.

The treatment: exercise.

"It's become clear that this is a good intervention, particularly for mild to moderate depression," says Jasper Smits, a psychologist at Southern Methodist University in Dallas [Texas]. Exercise as an anxiety treatment is less well-studied but looks helpful, he says.

It's no secret that exercise often boosts mood: The runner's high is legendary, and walkers, bikers, dancers and swimmers report their share of bliss.

Now, data pooled from many small studies suggest that in people diagnosed with depression or anxiety, the immediate mood boost is followed by longer-term relief, similar to that offered by medication and talk therapy, says Daniel Landers, a [retired] professor at Arizona State University.

And exercise seems to work better than relaxation, meditation, stress education and music therapy, Landers says.

"Most physicians and therapists are aware of the effects," says Chad Rethorst, a researcher at the University of Texas Southwestern Medical Center in Dallas. "But they may not be comfortable prescribing it."

Smits and another researcher, Michael Otto of Boston University, are on a mission to change that. The two have written a guidebook for mental-health professionals and are working on guides for primary care physicians and consumers.

Ideally, Smits says, depressed or anxious people would get written exercise prescriptions, complete with suggested "doses" and strategies for getting started and sticking with the program.

*this would be the last one and that he'd freeze up completely, bolt from the stage, and never be able to speak again. Finally, José told Mr. Dailey, one of his favorite teachers, about his fears. José was totally surprised*

One thing that helps people keep up this therapy, he says, is the immediate boost that many report. The same can't be said of taking pills, he says.

**Questions still to be answered**

But Smits and other exercise-as-treatment enthusiasts are quick to say that medications and psychotherapy are good treatments, too, and can be combined with exercise. "They work well," Smits says. "But too few people get them, and few get them in the doses that are needed."

Many people who start talk therapy or medications soon stop using them because of costs, side effects, inconvenience or other factors. In short-term studies, at least as many people stick with exercise as with drugs, Rethorst says. Not known, he says, is "how this will translate into the real world."

**Other remaining questions:**

- What kind of exercise works? Most studies have focused on aerobic exercise, such as running and walking, but have not ruled out strength training or other regimens.

- How much is needed? At least one study shows results from the amount recommended for physical health: 150 minutes of moderate exercise (such as brisk walking) or 75 minutes of vigorous exercise (such as running) each week.

- How does it help? Does it boost certain brain chemicals? Induce deeper sleep? Give patients a sense of action and accomplishment?

- Can it prevent initial bouts or recurrences of depression and anxiety?

That seems likely, says Michelle Riba, a psychiatrist who works with cancer patients and others at the University of Michigan. She prescribes exercise to depressed patients as part of a long-term plan for healthier living that includes sleep, eating and, in many cases, weight loss. Exercise can be especially important, she says, for patients taking antidepressant medications that cause weight gain.

"I don't think exercise will ever be the only treatment, but it may be a major part of preventing recurrences," she says. "It should be part of everybody's plan of health."

—Kim Painter

---

**Blues busters**

Can you walk away the blues? Quite possibly. Or you could try:

- Biking
- Jogging
- Swimming
- Tennis
- Basketball
- Dancing
- Inline skating
- Whatever form of moderate to vigorous exercise you like

---

*when the teacher told him he'd had similar fears. He spoke smoothly and confidently before the class, seemingly without a trace of nervousness. Mr. Dailey invited him to the local community Toastmasters Club. This is an international organization that meets all over the world to improve public speaking skills. As they attend regular meetings, members become more comfortable speaking in front of groups by speaking in the supportive environment of the Toastmasters group. José also saw a therapist who helped him confront and challenge his negative thoughts and beliefs. He realized that most of what he feared never happened. Even when negative things did happen—such as saying the wrong thing or leaving out some critical point—no one seemed to notice but him. When he lost a debate or a speech didn't go as smoothly as he'd planned, he examined his feelings and realized he didn't feel nearly as bad as he thought he would. The dread of losing or slipping up was worse than actually slipping up!*

## HOLLY: SPECIFIC PHOBIA

*As long as Holly could stay away from bees, she had been fine. It had even been funny at times. She forced herself to laugh after screaming at the sight of a bee in her neighbor's yard. Holly wasn't sure what she'd do if she'd found one in her yard! But then she'd met Jordon. If she wanted to join him in the things he enjoyed, Holly knew she'd better conquer her fear of bees. He liked to hike, rock climb, and fish. Jordon was understanding and helped Holly overcome her fears. First, they looked at pictures of bees. He spoke glowingly of their many fine attributes. You'd think they were his friends! Then they watched TV documentaries featuring bees and other stinging insects. When she felt comfortable viewing them in books and on TV, Holly and Jordan went to the home of a local beekeeper. There, Holly could directly confront her fear of bees in a controlled environment. First, she stood 20 feet (6 meters) from a beehive (with protective clothing on) and gradually inched up until she was only a foot (0.3 m) away from the hive.*

*Finally, Jordon asked the beekeeper if Holly could actually place her gloved hand on the hive. Holly didn't like touching the hive, but by then, she didn't fear the bees either. Jordon also helped her learn what to do in case she was stung by a bee. She replaced her irrational fears with rational beliefs. Now Holly has a healthy respect for bees, but no fear of them. She enjoys rock climbing and hiking but finds fishing boring. Jordon helped her realize she was severely restricting her life because she wouldn't go places where she might encounter bees.*

## JAKE: OBSESSIVE-COMPULSIVE DISORDER

*Anxiety was Jake's constant companion. The world seemed like a dangerous place. He worried about getting a disease and then contaminating someone in his family. By the time he started treatment, Jake was washing his hands one hundred times a day and showering for thirty minutes three times a day. He still didn't feel clean. Sometimes he washed his hands or showered just because a thought popped into his head and he felt unclean, contaminated. He felt as if the only way to feel clean again and to rid himself of the thought that he could be responsible for making someone else sick was to wash his hands or take a shower. Medication helped reduce Jake's obsessive thoughts about feeling unclean and spreading disease to others. After a few weeks, the urge to wash his hands and shower became weaker and he was better able to participate in cognitive behavioral therapy. He was able to reduce the number of times he washed his hands and showered and eventually stopped washing and showering in response to the obsessive thoughts. Jake learned to recognize the obsessive thoughts about being unclean and spreading disease as symptoms of his OCD, as false alarms, and to successfully resist the urges to wash.*

## PAUL: POST-TRAUMATIC STRESS DISORDER

*To his community and his family, especially to his sister and little brothers, Paul was a hero. Awakened by his dog, King, he alerted the rest of the*

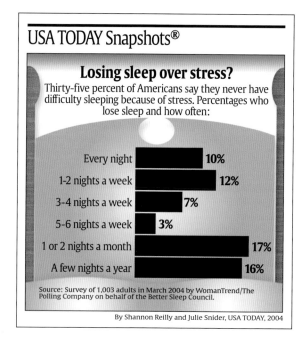

## USA TODAY Snapshots®

### Losing sleep over stress?

Thirty-five percent of Americans say they never have difficulty sleeping because of stress. Percentages who lose sleep and how often:

| | |
|---|---|
| Every night | 10% |
| 1-2 nights a week | 12% |
| 3-4 nights a week | 7% |
| 5-6 nights a week | 3% |
| 1 or 2 nights a month | 17% |
| A few nights a year | 16% |

Source: Survey of 1,003 adults in March 2004 by WomanTrend/The Polling Company on behalf of the Better Sleep Council.

By Shannon Reilly and Julie Snider, USA TODAY, 2004

family and saved them from the fire that destroyed his family home and that took his other sister's life. Paul didn't feel like a hero, however. His physical wounds healed, but the emotional scars only seemed to worsen. He was anxious and withdrawn, worried about his surviving sister and brothers. Paul checked the smoke detector daily, still not sure it was working properly. He stayed up late to avoid the nightmares he had about the fire, yet he couldn't remember much about it during the day. Paul's father also struggled with nightmares after the fire. He felt useless and depressed because he needed the disability payments he received as a result of his injuries. Recognizing that they needed help coping with the aftereffects of the fire, Paul and his father sought counseling together. This provided a safe environment for them to discuss what happened during the fire and how it had changed their family. They were able to express their fears, feelings, and thoughts and to frame themselves as "regular people" instead of as heroes.

## ROSA: ACUTE STRESS DISORDER

After Rosa was mugged, she withdrew from her usual activities, staying home, mostly in her room. Her family was supportive and encouraged her to talk about what happened. They discussed precautions they all could take to prevent such things from happening again. Eventually, she recognized that the mugging was just a random act that she *couldn't have prevented. She certainly wasn't going to let some mugger prevent her from enjoying life. Rosa recognized her need to spend more time with friends and family, relaxing and pursuing what mattered the most to her. She took a fresh look at her goals. After graduation from high school, she planned to enroll in nursing school. She talked with her school counselor about what she should be doing to increase her chances of getting scholarships. After applying to volunteer at the local hospital and obtaining application forms for several scholarships, Rosa felt more in control of her life and more confident about the future.*

## ELIZABETH: GENERAL ANXIETY DISORDER

*When her doctor informed her that her headaches were common migraines, Elizabeth breathed a sigh of relief. She worried herself sick over everything. It was as if her brain seemed to always be on, geared up for every event and situation in her life to go wrong, with emotions that were almost out of control. In treatment, her doctor taught her the skills to deal with the anxiety and stress that is part of daily living. Cognitive behavioral therapy helped her challenge automatic thoughts and beliefs instead of jumping to fearful conclusions. She examined her lifestyle and realized that the coffee drinks she downed every day were contributing to anxiety. Daily exercise, regular healthy eating habits, and taking the time to read a favorite book every day reduced her stress tremendously.*

Being diagnosed with an anxiety disorder can be devastating. Imagine feeling anxious, fearful, worried, perhaps even depressed and believing that you face a lifetime of always feeling the same way. Twenty-first century treatments offer tremendous hope for people with anxiety disorders. Once people learn and master skills such as the ones you've read about in this book, they can emerge healthier and more able to manage the challenges of life.

# GLOSSARY

**acute stress disorder:** a psychiatric disorder characterized by distressing psychological and physical symptoms following exposure to a traumatic event. The symptoms subside in less than one month.

**adrenaline:** also called epinephrine, a hormone produced by the adrenal gland in response to stress. Together with noradrenaline, it causes an increase in heart rate, blood pressure, mental activity, blood flow to the muscles, and metabolism. This prepares a person to deal with stress or perceived threats.

**agoraphobia:** an abnormal fear of being in open or public places; a psychiatric disorder in which a person's fear results in the avoidance of many situations and places that the person considers to be unsafe

**antidepressants:** medications that are designed to ease the symptoms of depressive illness. They are also known to be effective in relieving the symptoms of various anxiety disorders.

**anxiety:** an excessive, out-of-proportion response to a vague, ill-defined, future-oriented threat. It is often accompanied by physiological signs, doubt about the reality and nature of the threat, and self-doubt about one's ability to cope with the threat.

**anxiety disorder:** a psychiatric disorder in which anxiety is the predominant symptom

**benzodiazepines:** a group of medications that produce calming effects by enhancing the action of the neurotransmitter gamma-aminobutyric acid

**cognitive behavioral therapy (CBT):** a psychologically based therapy that includes strategies for helping people modify behavior and change dysfunctional beliefs that sustain anxiety and depressive symptoms

**cognitive strategies:** therapeutic techniques that focus on identifying faulty automatic beliefs and the negative thoughts that result from them and then directly challenging and testing them. Further techniques are used to replace them with accurate, positive, and functional beliefs and thoughts.

**compulsions:** repetitive behaviors or mental acts, often performed in an effort to diminish or neutralize the anxiety and distress brought on by the obsessive thoughts of obsessive-compulsive disorder

**depression:** an emotional state characterized by persistent and strong feelings of sadness, helplessness, and hopelessness; crying or frequent tearfulness; lack of energy; loss of interest in normal activities and pursuits; impaired appetite; weight loss or gain; impaired sleep; and suicidal feelings or thoughts.

**distress:** mental or physical strain brought about by pain, trouble, or worry; negative stress that is a result of a negative event in a person's life. Examples are being fired from a job, failing a test, getting a speeding ticket, and having a serious illness.

**dopamine:** a neurotransmitter that is involved in the control of movement and the sensation of pleasure

**eustress:** positive stress that is a result of a positive event in a person's life. Examples are exercise, cheering a favorite team, getting together with friends, and other enjoyable activities.

**exposure and response prevention ERP:** also called exposure and response ritual prevention, a behavior therapy technique in which a person confronts a feared situation by doing the actions or thinking the thoughts that create discomfort or fear. At the same time, the patient is required to refrain from doing the usual behavioral ritual usually employed to reduce the discomfort.

**fear:** a feeling of agitation and apprehension as a response to a well-defined danger, a specific object, or a particular situation

**fight-or-flight response:** a set of specific physiological changes, such as elevated heart rate and blood pressure, shortness of breath, and muscle tension, that occur in response to a perceived threat.

**gamma-aminobutyric acid (GABA):** a neurotransmitter that helps decrease brain activity. Some medications produce a calming effect through their influence on GABA.

**generalized anxiety disorder (GAD):** a psychiatric disorder characterized by a pattern of frequent, persistent worry and anxiety about several events or activities causing significant distress or impairment

**neurotransmitters:** chemicals in the brain that enable the transmission of electrical impulses between nerve cells, thus enabling communication between those nerve cells. They are vital to many physiological and psychological processes necessary for our survival.

**noradrenaline:** also called norepinephrine, a hormone and neurotransmitter produced by the adrenal glands and also secreted from nerve endings. A precursor to adrenaline, it works with adrenaline to cause an increase in heart rate, blood pressure, mental activity, blood flow to the muscles, and metabolism. This prepares a person to deal with stress or perceived threats.

**obsessions:** persistent, unwanted, irrational impulses, ideas, images, or thoughts that intrude into a person's mind, often causing intense anxiety and distress

**obsessive-compulsive disorder (OCD):** a neurobehavioral disorder in which people have obsessions and/or compulsions that are time consuming, distressing, or interfere with normal routines, relationships with others, or daily functioning

**panic attack:** a frightening experience of brief but very intense fear that occurs "out of the blue" and is accompanied by physical symptoms, such as elevated heart rate, shortness of breath, dizziness, sweating, and nausea

**panic disorder:** a disorder in which a person has brief episodes (panic attacks) of intense fear accompanied by physical symptoms, such as elevated heart rate, shortness of breath, dizziness, sweating, and nausea. The person also has an ongoing preoccupation with the fear of having another panic attack in the future.

**Pediatric Autoimmune Neuropsychiatric Disorders Associated with Streptococci (PANDAS):** a psychiatric disorder such as OCD, most often seen in children, which is the result of the body producing antibodies against streptococci bacteria that attack certain key areas deep within the brain

**post-traumatic stress disorder (PTSD):** a psychiatric disorder characterized by highly distressing psychological and physical symptoms following exposure to a traumatic event involving extreme danger to oneself or others

**relaxation response:** a state of deep relaxation with reduced heart rate, respiration, blood pressure, and muscle tension brought on by specific techniques of self-regulation, such as deep breathing, hypnosis, yoga, meditation, or progressive muscle relaxation

**selective serotonin reuptake inhibitors (SSRIs):** a group of antidepressants that work by increasing the amount of serotonin available to the nerve cells in the brain

**serotonin:** a neurotransmitter that is vital to the brain's capacity to properly regulate moods and control hunger, sleep, and aggression. An imbalance of serotonin contributes to anxiety and major mood disorders.

**social phobia:** also called social anxiety disorder, or SAD, a psychiatric disorder characterized by severe anxiety in social situations. People with social phobia fear that the scrutiny of others will result in their being horribly embarrassed or humiliated, or that others will think they're stupid, weak, or crazy.

**stage fright:** a phrase commonly used to describe social phobia that is associated with musical or other artistic-performing fears

**stress:** a state of mental, emotional, and/or physical strain or tension resulting from very demanding circumstances or psychological pressures

**stress management:** the active practice of a set of methods and techniques that promote the effective coping with the stressors of daily living and combat stress-related diseases, such as high blood pressure, diabetes, or heart disease

# RESOURCES

These organizations can provide further information about anxiety disorders. They may be able to provide the names of local doctors and therapists who have identified themselves as professionals who treat anxiety disorders. They don't always track the treatment practices of the professionals, however. Being on a list does not necessarily mean that a professional is competent to treat anxiety disorders, only that he or she has indicated an expertise or interest in the treatment of one or more anxiety disorders.

**Anxiety Disorders Association of America (ADAA)**
**Department A, 6000 Executive Boulevard**
**8730 Georgia Ave.**
**Silver Spring, MD 20910**
**240-485-1001**
**http://www.adaa.org**

**Association for Behavioral and Cognitive Therapies (ABCT)**
**305 Seventh Avenue, 16th Fl.**
**New York, NY 10001-6008**
**212-647-1890**
**http://www.abct.org**

**International Foundation for Research and Education on Depression (iFred)**
**PO Box 17598**
**Baltimore, MD 21297-1598**
**1-800-442-4673**
**http://www.ifred.org**

International OCD Foundation, Inc. (IOCDF)
PO Box 961029
Boston, MA 02196
617-973-5801
http://www.ocfoundation.org

Obsessive Action (OA)
Suite 506-507, Davina House, 137-149
Goswell Road, London EC1V 7ET
0845 390 6232, 020 7253 2664
http://www.ocdaction.org.uk

Obsessive-Compulsive Information Center
Madison Institute of Medicine, Inc.
6515 Grand Teton Plaza, Suite 100
Madison, WI 53719
608-827-2470
http://www.miminc.org

# SOURCE NOTES

46   Winston S. Churchill. *Memoirs of the Second World War.* (1959; repr. Boston: Houghton Mifflin Company, 1991), 394.

46   Eleanor Roosevelt. *You Learn by Living: Eleven Keys for a More Fulfilling Life.* (New York: Harper Perennials, 2011), 29.

58–59   Bruce Hyman, Ph.D. and Cherry Pedrick. *The OCD Workbook: Your Guide to Breaking Free from Obsessive-Compulsive Disorder*, 3rd ed. (Oakland: New Harbinger Publications, 2010), 32–33.

# SELECTED BIBLIOGRAPHY

American Psychiatric Association, *Diagnostic and Statistical Manual of Mental Disorders.* 4th ed. Washington, DC: American Psychiatric Association, 2000.

Antony, Martin M., and Richard P. Swinson. *The Shyness and Social Anxiety Workbook: Proven Techniques for Overcoming Your Fears.* Oakland, CA: New Harbinger Publications, 2000.

Barlow, D. H. *Anxiety and Its Disorders.* New York: Guilford Press, 2002.

Bourne, Edmund. *The Anxiety and Phobia Workbook.* 3rd ed. Oakland, CA: New Harbinger Publications, 2000.

Davidson, Jonathan, and Henry Dreher. *The Anxiety Book: Developing Strength in the Face of Fear.* New York: Riverhead Books, 2003.

Hyman, Bruce M., and Cherry Pedrick. *The OCD Workbook: Your Guide to Breaking Free from Obsessive-Compulsive Disorder.* 3rd ed. Oakland: New Harbinger Publications, 2010.

——. *Obsessive-Compulsive Disorder.* Minneapolis: Twenty-First Century Books, 2011.

# FURTHER READING

**For Young Readers and Teens**
Bell, J., and M. Jenike. *When in Doubt, Make Belief: An OCD-Inspired Approach to Living with Uncertainty.* Novato, CA: New World Library. 2009.

Bourne, Edmund. *The Anxiety and Phobia Workbook.* 5th ed. Oakland: New Harbinger Publications, 2011.

Burns, David D. *The Feeling Good Handbook.* Rev. ed. New York: Plume, 1999.

Claiborn, James, and Cherry Pedrick. *The Habit Change Workbook: How to Break Bad Habits and Form Good Ones.* Oakland: New Harbinger Publications, 2001.

Dayhoff, Signe A. *Diagonally Parked in a Parallel Universe: Working Through Social Anxiety.* Placitas, NM: Effectiveness-Plus Publications, 2000.

Hyman, Bruce M., and T. DuFrene. *Coping with OCD-Practical Strategies for Living Well with OCD.* Oakland: New Harbinger Publications. 2008.

Lohmann, Raychelle Cassada. *The Anger Workbook for Teens: Activities to Help You Deal with Anger and Frustration*. Oakland: New Harbinger Publications, 2009.

Osborn, I. *Can Christianity Cure Obsessive-Compulsive Disorder? A Psychiatrist Explores the Role of Faith in Treatment*. Grand Rapids: Baker Academic and Brazos Press, 2008.

Schab, Lisa M. *The Anxiety Workbook for Teens: Activities to Help You Deal with Anxiety and Worry*. Oakland: New Harbinger Publications, 2008.

———. *Beyond the Blues: A Workbook to Help Teens Overcome Depression*. Oakland: New Harbinger Publications, 2008.

**For Parents and Family Members**
Chansky, Tamar E. *Freeing Your Child from Anxiety: Powerful, Practical Solutions to Overcome Your Child's Fears, Worries, and Phobias*. New York: Broadway Books, 2004.

———. *Freeing Your Child from Negative Thinking: Powerful, Practical Strategies to Build a Lifetime of Resilience, Flexibility, and Happiness*. Cambridge, MA: Da Capo Press, [year of pub to come].

———. *Freeing Your Child from Obsessive-Compulsive Disorder: A Powerful, Practical Program for Parents of Children and Adolescents*. New York: Three Rivers Press, 2001.

Fitzgibbons, Lee, and Cherry Pedrick. *Helping Your Child with OCD: A Workbook for Parents of Children with Obsessive-Compulsive Disorder*. Oakland, CA: New Harbinger Publications, 2003.

March, John S. *Talking Back to OCD: The Program That Helps Kids and Teens Say "No Way"—and Parents Say "Way to Go."* New York: Guilford Press, 2006.

Rapee, Ronald, Susan Spence, Vanessa Cobham, and Ann Wignall. *Helping Your Anxious Child: A Step-by-Step Guide for Parents*. Oakland: New Harbinger Publications, 2000.

Wagner, Aureen Pinto. *Worried No More: Help and Hope for Anxious Children*. Rochester, NY: Lighthouse Press, 2002.

**For Teachers**
Dornbush, Marilyn, and Sheryl Pruitt. *Teaching the Tiger, a Handbook for Individuals Involved in the Education of Students with Attention Deficit Disorders, Tourette Syndrome or Obsessive-Compulsive Disorder*. Duarte, CA: Hope Press, 1993.

# WEBSITES

**Center for Psychiatric Rehabilitation**
**http://www.bu.edu/cpr/jobschool**

This is a website for people with a psychiatric condition that addresses issues and reasonable accommodations related to work and school, including information about the Americans with Disabilities Act (ADA), links to other school and work-related sites, and advice for coping at school and work.

**Cherry Pedrick's Website**
**http://CherryPedrick.com**

This is the official website of Cherry Pedrick, registered nurse and coauthor of this book.

**Internet Mental Health**
**http://www.mentalhealth.com/**

This is a great site for finding more information about anxiety disorders and mental illness.

**National Alliance on Mental Illness (NAMI)**
**http://www.nami.org**

NAMI is a national organization with affiliates in every state and more than eleven hundred communities with the mission of support, education, advocacy, and research for people living with mental illness. The website has information on OCD and other disorders, including interactive bulletin boards and links to state NAMI affiliates. Also included are Child and Teen Support, Veterans Resources, Multicultural Action Center, and FaithNet.

**National Institute of Mental Health (NIMH)**
**Science Writing, Press, and Dissemination Branch**
**http://www.nimh.nih.gov**

The NIMH is a component of the U.S. Department of Health and Human Services. The NIMH's mission is to reduce the burden of mental illness and behavioral disorders through research on mind, brain, and behavior. The website provides access to professional journals and the latest research and statistics.

**National Suicide Prevention Lifeline**
**www.suicidepreventionlifeline.org/**

This site has information about suicide and a search tool for finding a crisis center near you. There is also tool-free number for those in crisis or thinking about suicide. **1-800-273-TALK (8255)**, a free, 24-hour hotline available to anyone in suicidal crisis or emotional distress. Your call will be routed to the nearest crisis center to you. Or visit their website at www.suicidepreventionlifeline.org/

**OCD Resource Center of Florida**
**http://www.ocdhope.com**

This is the official website of Dr. Bruce Hyman, coauthor of this book. specific phobia: a psychiatric disorder involving an excessive or unreasonable fear of one particular type of object or situation.

LERNER

SOURCE

Expand learning beyond the printed book. Download free, complementary educational resources for this book from our website, www.lerneresource.com.

# INDEX

# ABOUT THE AUTHORS

Bruce M. Hyman, Ph.D., LCSW, is in private practice in Hollywood/Fort Lauderdale, Florida, and is the director of the OCD Resource Center of Florida. He is the coauthor of *The OCD Workbook: Your Guide to Breaking Free from Obsessive-Compulsive Disorder, 3rd edition; Obsessive-Compulsive Disorder;* and *Coping with OCD: Practical Strategies for Living Well with OCD.* Dr. Hyman specializes in the cognitive behavioral treatment of adults and children with OCD and other anxiety disorders.

Cherry Pedrick, R.N., is a registered nurse and a freelance writer living in Lacey, Washington. With Dr. Hyman, she is the coauthor of *The OCD Workbook: Your Guide to Breaking Free from Obsessive-Compulsive Disorder, 3rd edition,* and *Obsessive-Compulsive Disorder.* Cherry Pedrick is also the coauthor of *The Habit Change Workbook: How to Break Bad Habits and Form New Ones, The BDD Workbook: Overcome Body Dysmorphic Disorder and Body Image Obsessions, Helping Your Child with OCD,* and *Loving Someone with OCD.*

# PHOTO ACKNOWLEDGMENTS

The images in this book are used with the permission of: © George Doyle/Stockbyte/ Getty Images, pp. 1, 3; © Véronique Burger/Photo Researchers, Inc., p. 5; © Katye Martens/USA TODAY, p. 8; © Laura Westlund/Independent Picture Service, p. 28; © Josh Anderson/USA TODAY, p. 37; © Robert Deutsch/USA TODAY, p. 42; © Judy G. Rolfe/USA TODAY, p. 55; © Stockbyte/Getty Images, p. 64; ©Christina Kennedy/ DK Stock/Getty Images, p. 67; © OJO Images/Getty Images, p. 70; ©Parrypix/ Dreamstime.com, p. 76; © Todd Plitt/USA TODAY, p. 78; © Tay Rees/Stone/Getty Images, p. 89.

Cover: © iStockphoto.com/Andrey Prokhorov (EKG); © George Doyle/Stockbyte/ Getty Images (anxious woman).

Main body text set in USA TODAY Roman 10/15.